AIM Higher!

ISAT Language Arts Review
Level C

Robert D. Shepherd

Victoria S. Fortune

aim higher!®
Great Source Education Group
Wilmington, MA

Editorial Staff

Dan Carsen
Victoria S. Fortune
Robert D. Shepherd
Barbara R. Stratton

Production & Design Staff

Kazuko Ashizawa
Paige Larkin

Cover Design

Seann Dwyer, Studio Montage, St. Louis

Cover Photo

©George Contorakes/CORBIS

Consultant

Jennifer Aldred

aim higher! More than just teaching to the test™

Trademarks and trade names are shown in this book strictly for illustrative purposes and are the property of their respective owners. The authors' references herein should not be regarded as affecting their validity.

Copyright © 2003 by Great Source Education Group, a division of Houghton Mifflin Company.
All rights reserved.

Great Source® and AIM Higher® are registered trademarks of Houghton Mifflin Company.

No part of this work may be reproduced or transmitted in any form or by any means, electronic or mechanical, including photocopying and recording, or by any information storage or retrieval system without the prior written permission of Great Source Education Group, a division of Houghton Mifflin Company, unless such copying is expressly permitted by federal copyright law. Address inquiries to: Permissions, Great Source Education Group, 181 Ballardvale Street, Wilmington, MA 01887.

First Edition

Printed in the United States of America

1 2 3 4 5 6 7 8 9 10   DBH   07 06 05 04 03

International Standard Book Number: 1-58171-453-X

Contents

Pretest 1

Unit 1 • Test-Taking Strategies 33
  First Encounter "Gerbil Genius" 34
    Chapter 1 This Is Only a Test • Taking Tests 38
      Understanding Tests 38
      Preparing for Tests 39
      Test-Taking Tips 43
    Chapter 2 ISAT for Reading and ISAT for Writing •
      Understanding Your State Tests 51

Unit 2 • Reading Skills Review 61
  First Encounter "Make Mine Milk" 62
    Chapter 3 Sound Off! • Sounds, Spellings, and Word Parts ... 69
      The Sounds and Spellings of Consonants 70
      The Sounds and Spelling of Vowels 76
      The Parts of Words 92
    Chapter 4 Talking Back to Books • Active Reading 99
      Reading Actively 100
      Before Reading 101
      During Reading 107
      After Reading 119
    Chapter 5 I Think I've Got It! • Reading Comprehension 122
      Pay Attention to What's Important 122
      Look for Main Ideas 125
      Look for Significant Details 129
      Look for Sequences 133
      Look for Causes and Effects 137
      Look for Context Clues 142
      Look for the Theme 146
    Chapter 6 The Truth and Then Some • Reading Nonfiction and Fiction ... 153
      Reading Nonfiction Actively 155
      Reading Fiction Actively 163
      The Sounds Writers Use 172

Unit 3 • Notetaking and Graphic Organizers ... 173
First Encounter "Gators and Crocs" ... 174
Chapter 7 Hold That Thought • Introduction to Notetaking ... 180
What Are Notes? ... 180
When to Take Notes ... 181
How to Take Notes ... 182
Symbols and Abbreviations ... 184
Chapter 8 Picture This! • Using Graphic Organizers ... 186
Making Word Webs ... 186
Making Timelines ... 188
Making Charts ... 190
Using Graphic Organizers for Notetaking ... 192

Unit 4 • Writing Skills Review ... 195
First Encounter "A Little World" (student essay) ... 197
Chapter 9 Step by Step • The Writing Process ... 200
Prewriting ... 202
Drafting ... 209
Revising ... 210
Proofreading ... 213
Publishing or Sharing ... 218
Chapter 10 Perfect Paragraphs • Main Ideas and Supporting Details ... 219
What Is a Paragraph? ... 219
Types of Paragraph ... 222
Writing Paragraphs for Tests ... 226
Chapter 11 Excellent Essays • Introduction, Body, and Conclusion ... 228
Planning an Essay ... 231
Writing the Introduction ... 236
Writing the Body of the Essay ... 240
Writing the Conclusion ... 243

Unit 5 • Guided Writing Practice ... 245
Chapter 12 Guided Practice • Writing about Literature ... 245
Chapter 13 Guided Practice • Writing Narrative Nonfiction ... 250
Chapter 14 Guided Practice • Writing Expository, or Informative, Nonfiction ... 253
Chapter 15 Guided Practice • Writing Persuasive Nonfiction ... 256

Posttest ... 259
Glossary ... 291
Index ... 299

Pretest

ISAT for Reading
ISAT for Writing

Pretest

ISAT for Reading and Writing

This Pretest is like the Illinois Standards Achievement Test (ISAT) for Reading and the Illinois Standards Achievement Test (ISAT) for Writing. The Pretest is organized as follows:

Part 1: ISAT for Reading

Session 1: Fourteen word-analysis questions and one reading selection with multiple-choice questions

Session 2: One reading selection with multiple-choice questions and an extended-response question

Session 3: One reading selection with multiple-choice questions and an extended-response question

Part 2: ISAT for Writing

Response to one writing prompt chosen by the student

PART 1: ISAT for Reading
SESSION 1

ISAT for Reading: SESSION 1

Word Analysis

Directions Your teacher will read each question. Fill in the bubble of the letter next to the correct answer. All of these questions have only one correct answer. Do not begin until your teacher gives you directions.

1. *The students reported to the **gym**.*

   Which word <u>begins</u> with the same sound as **gym**?
   - Ⓐ give
   - Ⓑ guess
   - Ⓒ giant
   - Ⓓ gone

2. *Do not step on the **crack** in the sidewalk!*

   Which word <u>begins</u> with the same sounds as **crack**?
   - Ⓐ cool
   - Ⓑ climb
   - Ⓒ choose
   - Ⓓ cry

3. Which word has the same "i" sound as the letter "i" in **pig**?
   - Ⓐ ice
   - Ⓑ fill
   - Ⓒ wife
   - Ⓓ fire

4. What does **unopened** mean?
   - Ⓐ already opened
   - Ⓑ almost opened
   - Ⓒ not opened
   - Ⓓ completely opened

GO ON

ISAT Reading and Writing Pretest 3

Pretest

5. What is the root of the word **dislike**?
   - Ⓐ is
   - Ⓑ dis
   - Ⓒ slike
   - Ⓓ like

6. What does the word **wonderful** mean?
   - Ⓐ without wonder
   - Ⓑ full of wonder
   - Ⓒ feeling wonder
   - Ⓓ one who wonders

7. *On the teacher's desk was a red* **rose.**

   Which word <u>begins</u> with the same sound as the "s" sound in **rose**?
   - Ⓐ sold
   - Ⓑ shoulder
   - Ⓒ scary
   - Ⓓ zoo

8. How many syllables are in the word **factory**?
   - Ⓐ one syllable
   - Ⓑ two syllables
   - Ⓒ three syllables
   - Ⓓ four syllables

9. *The skin of the hippo was really* **rough.**

   Which word <u>ends</u> with the same sound as the word **rough**?
   - Ⓐ through
   - Ⓑ moth
   - Ⓒ huff
   - Ⓓ ouch

**PART 1: ISAT for Reading
SESSION 1**

10. *Where is my other **shoe?***

    Which word <u>ends</u> with the same sound as the "sh" sound in the word **shoe**?

    Ⓐ nose
    Ⓑ bunch
    Ⓒ trash
    Ⓓ miss

11. *Josh stood in the **center** of the ring of kids.*

    Which word <u>begins</u> with the same sound as **center**?

    Ⓐ carpool
    Ⓑ ship
    Ⓒ catbox
    Ⓓ sand

12. What does **incomplete** mean?

    Ⓐ very complete
    Ⓑ too complete
    Ⓒ almost complete
    Ⓓ not complete

13. Which word has the same sound as the letters "ou" in **shout**?

    Ⓐ court
    Ⓑ short
    Ⓒ cow
    Ⓓ boot

14. Which word has the same sound as the letters "oo" in **root**?

    Ⓐ hook
    Ⓑ lot
    Ⓒ look
    Ⓓ flute

GO ON

ISAT Reading and Writing Pretest 5

Pretest

ISAT for Reading: SESSION 1, continued

Directions *This selection is about a great athlete. Read the selection. Then answer multiple-choice questions 15 through 28.*

A True Champion
by Robert Kaufman

Portraits of Althea Gibson

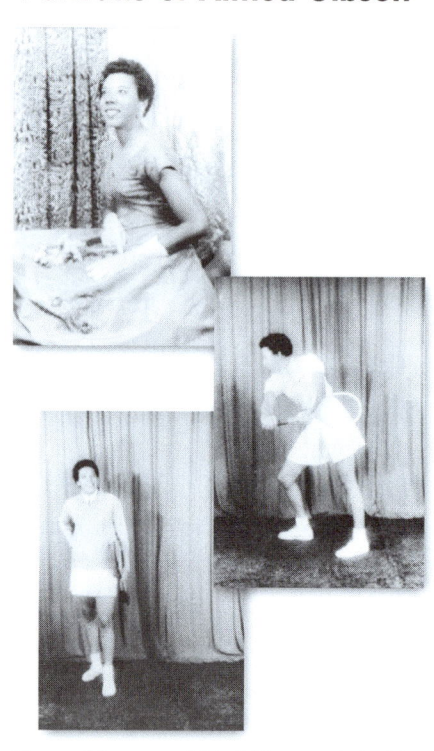

Library of Congress, Prints & Photographs Division [LOT 12735, nos. 413, 420, 418].

Althea Gibson was born in South Carolina in 1927. Her parents worked on a cotton farm. When Althea was very young, her family moved to New York City. They lived in a part of New York called Harlem.

Althea loved to play sports as a child. She grew tall, and she was strong. At first, she liked to play basketball. Then, she began to play tennis. She played in matches held for African American tennis players.

For many years in the United States, whites and African Americans were kept apart. This was called segregation. In many communities, schools were segregated. Also, African Americans could not drink from the same water fountains as white people. Nor could they use bathrooms that were used by whites. African Americans did not have many rights or opportunities at this time. In the world of sports, it was the same. African Americans were not allowed to compete with white people in sports.

At this time, in the 1950s, Althea Gibson was one of the best amateur female tennis players. In sports, an amateur is someone who does not get paid to play. She took a brave step forward and asked if she could play in the top event for American tennis players. This was the U.S. Nationals. The event had special rules.

**PART 1: ISAT for Reading
SESSION 1**

One rule was that African American women were not allowed to play. Gibson was told that she could not play.

Then a white player name Alice Marble spoke up for Gibson. Marble was one of the top players in the sport at the time. She felt that Gibson deserved a chance to play because she was one of the best players in the country.

Marble's words made a difference. She helped change the course of women's tennis. Gibson was allowed to compete in the U.S. Nationals. She won her first match. This made her the first African American woman to win a match in this event.

Gibson lost the second match. Her opponents were very strong players. However, Gibson did not give up. She realized that she needed to improve her game. She also continued to face problems because of her race. Many tennis clubs still refused to let her play because she was African American.

Gibson worked hard at practicing her tennis. After a few years, her game greatly improved. In 1956, she won her first major tennis tournament in France. The next year, she became the first African American to win at Wimbledon, in England. Wimbledon is the most famous championship event held in tennis. This same year, she was named Woman Athlete of the Year. Gibson had broken down the barriers of race within the tennis world.

Gibson decided to retire from tennis in 1958. She went on to play professional golf. Once again, she paved the way for African Americans in this sport. In 1963, Gibson became the first African American woman to play professional golf.

Althea Gibson was much like Jackie Robinson. He was the first African American to play major league baseball. Gibson was a pioneer for black women in sports. Thanks to her physical ability and her determination, she was able to pave the way for other world-class African American athletes. Serena Williams, Venus Williams, and Tiger Woods are only a few to follow in her path.

Pretest

Directions *For each question, choose the best answer. You may look back at the selection at any time.*

"A True Champion," by Robert Kaufman

15. Where did Althea Gibson grow up?
    - Ⓐ South Carolina
    - Ⓑ New York
    - Ⓒ England
    - Ⓓ France

16. What helped Gibson become a good tennis player?
    - Ⓐ She played professional golf.
    - Ⓑ She lived in New York.
    - Ⓒ She was tall and strong.
    - Ⓓ She played basketball.

17. How did segregation affect most African Americans?
    - Ⓐ Segregation had no effect on them.
    - Ⓑ They were allowed to do whatever they wanted.
    - Ⓒ They were not allowed to do many things they wanted to.
    - Ⓓ They went to the same schools and clubs as white people.

18. What happened when Gibson first tried to enter the U.S. Nationals?
    - Ⓐ The other tennis players were angry because she won.
    - Ⓑ She was not allowed to play because she was not good enough.
    - Ⓒ She decided to retire from tennis because she lost.
    - Ⓓ She was told she could not play because of the color of her skin.

**PART 1: ISAT for Reading
SESSION 1**

19. Why did Alice Marble think that Gibson should play in the U.S. Nationals?
    - Ⓐ She felt that the best players should be able to compete, no matter what race they were.
    - Ⓑ She felt that Gibson did not have a chance to win.
    - Ⓒ She thought Gibson should take up golf instead.
    - Ⓓ She thought that anyone should be allowed to compete, even if he or she had no skill.

20. What happened the first time Gibson played in the U.S. Nationals?
    - Ⓐ She lost her first and second matches.
    - Ⓑ She won her first match but lost her second one.
    - Ⓒ She was defeated in the finals.
    - Ⓓ She became the U.S. champion.

21. Gibson's opponents at the U.S. Nationals were very strong. Who were her *opponents?*
    - Ⓐ her friends
    - Ⓑ the people who played against her
    - Ⓒ her brothers and sisters
    - Ⓓ the people who watched her play

22. What did Gibson learn from her first visit to the U.S. Nationals?
    - Ⓐ Serena Williams was a better tennis player.
    - Ⓑ Gibson was the best tennis player in the United States.
    - Ⓒ Gibson liked golf better than tennis.
    - Ⓓ Gibson needed to work to improve her tennis skills.

GO ON

Pretest

23. Where did Gibson win her first major event?
- Ⓐ Harlem
- Ⓑ England
- Ⓒ France
- Ⓓ The U.S. Nationals

24. What challenge did Gibson face when she tried to become a professional golfer?
- Ⓐ African Americans were not allowed to play pro golf.
- Ⓑ She needed to improve her game.
- Ⓒ She had never played golf before.
- Ⓓ She found that golf was really hard to play.

25. Which of the following is true of both Althea Gibson and Jackie Robinson?
- Ⓐ They both started their careers as tennis players.
- Ⓑ They were both born in South Carolina in 1927.
- Ⓒ They were both professional golfers who won major tournaments.
- Ⓓ They were both pioneers who paved the way for other African American athletes.

26. Althea Gibson helped to break down the barriers of race in the sports world. What is a *barrier*?
- Ⓐ something that keeps people apart
- Ⓑ a person who tends a goal
- Ⓒ a person who is good at a sport
- Ⓓ something that brings people together

PART 1: ISAT for Reading
SESSION 1

27. Which saying best describes Gibson's attitude toward her career?
   Ⓐ An apple a day keeps the doctor away.
   Ⓑ If at first you don't succeed, try, try again.
   Ⓒ A watched pot never boils.
   Ⓓ A penny saved is a penny earned.

28. Gibson was a pioneer for black women in sports. What is a *pioneer*?
   Ⓐ someone who likes sports
   Ⓑ someone who leads the way
   Ⓒ someone who has a different skin color
   Ⓓ someone who is afraid to try something new

End of PART 1: SESSION 1 STOP

Pretest

ISAT for Reading: SESSION 2

Directions This selection is about a girl who is determined to learn how to ride her bike. Read the selection. Then answer multiple-choice questions 29 through 48 and the extended-response question.

The Acorn and the Oak
by Mark Cheever

Robin Shulka couldn't have been happier. After months of begging her parents for a new bike, here it was at last. Nothing could be better than this new, bright red girl's bike with red and white streamers on the handlebars. Best of all, unlike her old bike, this one didn't have training wheels.

For a long time, Robin's brother Nick had made fun of her.

"Baby Robin has to ride with training wheels," he would say.

Listening to him made Robin really mad. He was three years older and had a green mountain bike with racing stripes. He rode his bike all around the neighborhood, and he did tricks on the bike, too. Robin had to make do with Nick's old bike, a rusted gray one with training wheels on the back. She hated having to ride an old boys' bike.

Sometimes Robin asked to go riding with Nick.

"No way," he always said. "You're too little and couldn't keep up." Then he would go off riding with his friends.

When Nick first started making fun of the training wheels on her old bike, Robin asked her father to take the wheels off.

"Not now," Dad said. "Wait till you're a little bit older."

Most of the summer went by. School started again. The leaves turned yellow and orange and red and started falling from the trees. The nights grew chilly.

Then, in mid-October, Robin came home from school and found the new bike waiting for her. It was a mountain bike, just like her brother's. Robin was very excited. Now she could ride just like the big kids. She hopped on the bike and tried to hold herself up. At once she toppled over, bike and all. Her brother, who was standing by, laughed.

"You'll never learn to ride. You're such a klutz," he said.

Their father, who was coming out of the house, heard what Nick said. "Come in the house, young man. I want to talk to you," Dad said. He grounded Nick for a whole week. During the week, Nick would have to stay inside and could not visit his friends. Worst of all, he wouldn't be able to ride his bike around the neighborhood. That was his punishment for making fun of his sister.

After talking to Nick, Dad went outside. Robin was sitting on the ground next to her bike, crying. Her knee was skinned where she had fallen. Dad went inside and got some medicine and sprayed it on the skinned knee. Then he grabbed the bike and told Robin to come with him.

Together, they walked to a nearby park. In the park were lots of dirt paths. The dirt on the paths was packed solid. Dad told Robin to get on the bike. He wanted her to try riding on the paths, where, if she fell, she would land on soft ground. But Robin was afraid of climbing on the bike again.

"Maybe Nick's right," she said. "Maybe I can't learn how to ride without training wheels." Then she started crying again.

Dad reached over and picked up an acorn from the ground. "Do you know what this is?" he asked.

"It's an acorn," said Robin, brushing tears from her face.

"Right. But it's also a seed. Do you see that tree up there?" Dad pointed at a huge oak tree that towered above their heads. "Given a little time, a tiny acorn grows into a large oak tree. Now, would it make sense for me to make fun of this acorn because it is not yet an oak?"

Pretest

54. By the end of the story, how does Will's attitude toward swimming change?
    - Ⓐ He enjoys it and knows that it is an important skill to have.
    - Ⓑ He is glad that he knows how, but he still doesn't enjoy it.
    - Ⓒ He loves it and wants to move to a place where there is more water.
    - Ⓓ His attitude toward swimming does not change at all.

55. How old is Will?
    - Ⓐ eleven
    - Ⓑ ten
    - Ⓒ nine
    - Ⓓ eight

56. Will says, "I tried to sound casual, but my voice cracked a little." What does *casual* mean in this sentence?
    - Ⓐ brittle and scratchy
    - Ⓑ calm and relaxed
    - Ⓒ nervous and scared
    - Ⓓ happy and energetic

57. Will pretends to be proud that he cannot swim. How does he really feel?
    - Ⓐ embarrassed
    - Ⓑ confident
    - Ⓒ happy
    - Ⓓ carefree

"Well, no," said Robin.

"Of course not," said Dad. "That's why I punished Nick. He's not dumb, but he said some really dumb things. He shouldn't make fun of you just because you are little. Everything and everyone grows at its own speed. Give a little thing enough time and space, and it can grow up to be pretty impressive."

Dad took Robin to the park three times during the next week. The first time they went, Robin kept falling off the bike. When Robin felt discouraged and wanted to give up, Dad would remind her of the acorn and the oak. The second time they went to the park, Robin rode a few feet without falling off. The third time they went, she rode all around the park by herself. She was very proud. Soon she was riding up and down the sidewalk in front of the house every day after school.

A couple of weeks went by. Nick came home from school one day and saw Robin riding on the sidewalk. "Hey, good job, little sister," he said. "Do you want to go to the church parking lot and ride around together?"

"Sure," said Robin.

"Listen, I am sorry about what I said," Nick told her.

"Don't mention it," said Robin. "You didn't know I was just an acorn."

Nick scratched his head. He didn't know what Robin meant. "Crazy kid," he thought, but they went off together and had a wonderful time.

PART 1: ISAT for Reading
SESSION 2

Directions For each question, choose the best answer. You may look back at the selection as often as necessary.

"The Acorn and the Oak," by Mark Cheever

29. What is this story mostly about?
    Ⓐ a seed that grows into a tree
    Ⓑ a girl who learns how to ride a bike
    Ⓒ a boy who teases his sister
    Ⓓ a father who likes to spend time with his children

30. What does Robin like "best of all" about her new bike?
    Ⓐ It is bright red.
    Ⓑ It has red and white streamers on the handlebars.
    Ⓒ It is a girl's bike.
    Ⓓ It does not have any training wheels.

31. Why won't Dad take the training wheels off of Robin's old bike?
    Ⓐ They are rusted to the frame and won't come off.
    Ⓑ He thinks she is too young to ride without training wheels.
    Ⓒ Her mother doesn't want Dad to take the training wheels off.
    Ⓓ He is too busy and does not have time to take them off.

32. Why does Nick get grounded?
    Ⓐ He refuses to take Robin to the park.
    Ⓑ He will not let Robin play with his friends.
    Ⓒ He will not share his mountain bike with Robin.
    Ⓓ He makes fun of Robin because she cannot ride a bike.

GO ON

Pretest

33. Which of the following happens first?
- Ⓐ Robin skins her knee.
- Ⓑ Robin gets a new bike.
- Ⓒ Nick and Robin go riding together.
- Ⓓ Dad tells Robin the story of the acorn and the oak.

34. Where did Dad take Robin to practice riding her bike?
- Ⓐ a church parking lot
- Ⓑ a quiet neighborhood street
- Ⓒ a nearby park
- Ⓓ the driveway

35. The story says Robin "toppled over, bike and all." What does *toppled* mean?
- Ⓐ jumped
- Ⓑ skipped
- Ⓒ rolled
- Ⓓ fell

36. What is the point of Dad's story about the acorn and the oak?
- Ⓐ Robin should forgive her brother for teasing her.
- Ⓑ Robin should learn about the way oak trees grow.
- Ⓒ Robin is small now, but soon she will grow bigger.
- Ⓓ Robin should laugh at herself when she falls off her bike.

37. Why does Dad point at a huge oak tree and not a small oak tree?
- Ⓐ He wants to show Robin the tree he planted.
- Ⓑ He wants to show Robin how big an oak can get.
- Ⓒ He wants to show Robin how funny the tree is.
- Ⓓ He wants to show Robin where he found the acorn.

**PART 1: ISAT for Reading
SESSION 2**

38. Robin's dad reminds her of the story of the acorn and the oak whenever she feels discouraged. What does *discouraged* mean?
    Ⓐ hopeful and excited
    Ⓑ ready to give up
    Ⓒ angry with someone
    Ⓓ sad and lonely

39. Why is Robin finally able to ride her bike?
    Ⓐ She keeps trying until she can do it.
    Ⓑ She has the training wheels to help her.
    Ⓒ Her brother gives her some tips to help her.
    Ⓓ She keeps watching how her father does it.

40. How does Robin feel when she learns to ride her new bike?
    Ⓐ a little scared
    Ⓑ very proud
    Ⓒ eager to show Nick
    Ⓓ bored

41. When Nick sees Robin riding up and down the sidewalk on her new bike, what does he do?
    Ⓐ He makes fun of her again.
    Ⓑ He asks her to go riding with his friends.
    Ⓒ He invites her to take a ride with him.
    Ⓓ He goes in the house to get Dad.

42. Over what length of time does the story take place?
    Ⓐ a few days
    Ⓑ a few weeks
    Ⓒ a few months
    Ⓓ a few years

GO ON

Pretest

43. What do you learn about Nick when he says, "Listen, I am sorry about what I said"?
    - Ⓐ Nick's father made him apologize.
    - Ⓑ Nick cares about his little sister's feelings.
    - Ⓒ Nick wants to borrow Robin's bike.
    - Ⓓ Nick still likes to tease Robin.

44. What does Robin mean when she says to Nick, "You didn't know I was just an acorn"?
    - Ⓐ Nick did not know that his little sister just needed time to learn how to ride a bike without training wheels.
    - Ⓑ Nick did not know his sister would be taller than he was when she grew up.
    - Ⓒ Nick did not know that he had made Robin cry when he made fun of her.
    - Ⓓ Nick did not know how to teach Robin to ride a bicycle without training wheels.

**PART 1: ISAT for Reading
SESSION 2**

45. Why does the author include the conversation between Robin and Nick at the end of the story?
    - Ⓐ to tell what Robin is going to do next
    - Ⓑ to show that Nick sees that Robin is more grown up
    - Ⓒ to tell what Robin's bicycle looks like
    - Ⓓ to explain why Dad took Robin to the park

46. What would be another possible title for this story?
    - Ⓐ "Robin Teaches Nick a Lesson"
    - Ⓑ "Dad Buys a Bike"
    - Ⓒ "Time to Grow"
    - Ⓓ "The Story of the Three Bikes"

47. Which word best describes Robin's dad?
    - Ⓐ strict
    - Ⓑ patient
    - Ⓒ angry
    - Ⓓ silly

48. Which of the following will Robin most likely do in the future?
    - Ⓐ refuse to speak to Nick again
    - Ⓑ give away her bright red bike
    - Ⓒ ride her bike in races
    - Ⓓ ride around the neighborhood with Nick

GO ON

ISAT Reading and Writing Pretest 19

Pretest

Extended-Response Question

49. How does Dad help Robin to learn how to ride her bike? Do you think she could have learned without his help?

_____
_____
_____
_____
_____
_____
_____
_____
_____
_____
_____
_____
_____

End of PART 1: SESSION 2

Note to Students: Your written response will be scored using a rubric like the one on page 54.

**PART 1: ISAT for Reading
SESSION 3**

ISAT for Reading: SESSION 3

Directions This selection is about a boy who learns how to swim. Read the selection. Then answer multiple-choice questions 50 through 69 and the extended-response question.

The Creek
by Will Renson

Where I live, it never rains. Well, almost never. Every once in a while it rains. One summer it rained and rained and rained. It rained till the ground couldn't soak up any more water. The dusty pastures turned to fields of mud. That was the summer my cousin Kirby came to stay with us. It was also the summer that I learned how to swim.

One scorching hot day, Kirby and I decided to go down to the creek. Whenever it got really hot, I liked to wade in the creek to cool off. But as we got to the top of the hill overlooking the creek bed, I gasped. The little trickle of water had become a river. It was three times as wide as usual. I had never seen the creek so high. I stood at the edge of the swirling water with my jaw hanging open. Then my foot slipped in the mud. I almost fell in. A shiver of fear shot up my back.

"What's the matter, Will?" Kirby chuckled. "You scared of the water?" Kirby was ten, a whole year older than I was.

"It's just...it looks kind of deep." I tried to sound casual, but my voice cracked a little.

GO ON

Pretest

"Don't you know how to swim?" Kirby asked, as if he had never heard of someone not knowing how to swim.

"No," I shot back. I pretended to be proud of it. In fact, I was embarrassed. I felt as if I were the only kid on the planet who didn't know how to swim. I knew I wasn't. None of my friends knew how to swim. But at that moment, I felt like a freak.

"Well," Kirby said as he kicked off his shoes. "You should learn. C'mon. I'll teach you." He peeled off his T-shirt and jumped into the creek.

"Um...I, uh, I don't know," I struggled to think of a reason to say no. The truth is, I was sort of scared of the water. It was fine when it only came up to my knees, but this was different. My head could go under. The thought of being all the way under the water made my heart beat fast. The only excuse I could think of was, "My parents might get mad."

"Why?" Kirby yelled from the water. "Look, it's not that deep." Kirby stood in the center of the creek. The water came just to his armpits. "My dad says everyone should know how to swim...for safety reasons."

"Well I better go ask my mom, just in case." I was trying to stall. I didn't really want to learn how to swim. I was hoping Mom would say it wasn't a good idea. Unfortunately, Mom thought it was a great idea.

"Everyone ought to know how to swim...for safety's sake," she said as she gathered up a bowl and strainer full of peas in pods. "I'll shell peas by the creek, so I can watch," she added cheerfully.

When we got back to the creek, we found Kirby lying in the grass, whistling. He jumped up when he saw us.

"Ready, Will?" he asked.

"Yeah, I guess so," I mumbled. I couldn't admit to Kirby that I was scared of the water.

"First rule," Kirby said, "is always keep your mouth shut. Pretend that it is glued shut. That way, you won't swallow any water..."

"Or any bugs," Mom added with a grin.

I gave her a dirty look.

Kirby laughed as he jumped into the water. I walked in slowly. The cool water felt great. I clamped my mouth shut and walked until the water was almost up to my chest.

"OK," Kirby said. "Now hold your nose and dunk your head under."

I tried to stay calm, but my heart was racing. "It's OK," I told myself. "You've got your feet on the ground. You can always stand up again." I took a deep breath and quickly dunked my head in the water.

Kirby laughed. "You didn't even get your hair wet. Go all the way under, and let your body go loose."

This time I let my body sink until my head was all the way under. I tried to relax. The water seemed to be holding me up. As I moved around, I felt as if I were going in slow motion. When I came back up, Kirby said I ought to be a good swimmer if I could hold my breath that long.

Next, he told me to take a deep breath and fall backward. "Arch your back. Push the back of your head into the water," he directed. When I did this, my body floated. It felt as if I were lying on a mattress, looking up at the sky. I could have floated like that all day. But Kirby yelled out, "Hey, you're floating away." I looked around and realized I was drifting downstream. I quickly stood up.

"See how the water holds you up," Kirby yelled. "Now, you're going to turn over and float like that on your stomach. It's a little harder on your stomach. You have to keep your head up, which makes your legs sink. But try to keep your body straight."

Pretest

He was right. My legs kept sinking. It was hard to keep them up. I wasn't even worrying about going under water, anymore. I was concentrating too hard on what Kirby was telling me to do.

"OK," Kirby said. "When I say go, you're going to start kicking your legs. At the same time, reach your arms out in front of you, one at a time, and pull the water towards you. Like this," he said as he showed me. "Go."

I tried to follow his directions. I reached out with my arms, but I forgot to kick. Then I sucked in a huge gulp of water. I came up coughing and sputtering.

"Good job with your arms," Kirby called out. "Don't forget to kick, though," he added. "And keep your mouth shut. It takes a little practice," he said.

After a couple of hours, I seemed to be getting the hang of it. Finally, Mom ordered me to get out, because she needed to go cook dinner. Kirby and I went swimming every day that week. By the end of the week, I could easily swim from one bank to the other and back again. Dad started calling me the little fish.

A few weeks later, I was riding my horse Rocky across the creek when a snake spooked him. He reared up, and I went flying into the creek. Luckily, I didn't hit my head on anything. I landed in the deepest part, where I couldn't stand up. I spluttered and started moving my arms and legs right away. If I hadn't known how to swim, I might have drowned. The way Kirby tells it, he saved my life. I guess, in a way, he did.

PART 1: ISAT for Reading
SESSION 3

Directions For each question, choose the best answer. You may look back at the selection as often as necessary.

"The Creek," by Will Renson

50. What is this story mostly about?
    - Ⓐ a boy who argues with his cousin
    - Ⓑ a creek that turns into a river
    - Ⓒ a boy who learns how to swim
    - Ⓓ a boy who learns how to ride horses

51. Why does the author tell readers that it rained a lot the summer that the story takes place?
    - Ⓐ to explain why the crops on the farm were very good that year
    - Ⓑ to explain why Mom has lots of peas to shell by the side of the creek
    - Ⓒ to explain why the creek is deep enough to make Will nervous
    - Ⓓ to explain why Will's jaw dropped open and let water and bugs in

52. What is one lesson that the story teaches?
    - Ⓐ No one who lives in the West knows how to swim.
    - Ⓑ Horses are afraid of snakes.
    - Ⓒ You shouldn't try something if it is scary.
    - Ⓓ Everyone should learn how to swim.

53. At the beginning of the story, how does Will feel about swimming?
    - Ⓐ It is one of his favorite pastimes.
    - Ⓑ He is eager to learn how to swim.
    - Ⓒ He is scared to learn how to swim.
    - Ⓓ He likes to swim every once in a while.

GO ON

PART 1: ISAT for Reading
SESSION 3

58. Why does Will go back to the house to tell his mother that Kirby is going to teach him how to swim?

   Ⓐ He knows that it is not safe to go swimming without an adult around.

   Ⓑ He hopes that his mother will not let him learn to swim in the creek.

   Ⓒ He wants her to watch and see what a good swimmer he has become.

   Ⓓ He thinks if his mother is there, Kirby will not play any tricks on him.

59. Why does Will's mother think Will should learn how to swim?

   Ⓐ for safety's sake

   Ⓑ to avoid mosquitoes

   Ⓒ for fun and for racing

   Ⓓ to cool off on hot days

60. What is the first rule about swimming that Kirby tells Will?

   Ⓐ Let your body sink.

   Ⓑ Keep your head up.

   Ⓒ Keep your mouth shut.

   Ⓓ Kick your legs.

61. Why does Kirby say that Will ought to be a good swimmer?

   Ⓐ because Will is very athletic and intelligent

   Ⓑ because Will can hold his breath for a long time

   Ⓒ because Kirby usually lies to make people feel good

   Ⓓ because Will likes to float and to feel the cool water

GO ON

Pretest

62. Which of the following words best describes Kirby?

- Ⓐ mean
- Ⓑ helpful
- Ⓒ greedy
- Ⓓ serious

63. Will says, "I tried to stay calm, but my heart was racing." What does *racing* mean in this sentence?

- Ⓐ staying calm
- Ⓑ running fast
- Ⓒ skipping
- Ⓓ beating fast

64. What is the worst thing that happens to Will while he is learning to swim?

- Ⓐ He gets in a big fight with Kirby.
- Ⓑ He cuts his foot on a sharp rock.
- Ⓒ He sucks in a huge gulp of water.
- Ⓓ His horse gets loose and runs away.

65. What does Will mean when he says, "It felt as if I were lying on a mattress"?

- Ⓐ that the water in the creek supported his body as if he were on a bed
- Ⓑ that the water in the creek was as soft as his bed
- Ⓒ that the water in the creek made him feel sleepy and relaxed
- Ⓓ that the water in the creek was too warm, just like his bedroom

PART 1: ISAT for Reading
SESSION 3

66. What happens last in the story?
    Ⓐ Will is thrown off his horse.
    Ⓑ Will almost falls into the creek.
    Ⓒ Will's mom comes down to the creek.
    Ⓓ Kirby offers to teach Will to swim.

67. By the end of the story, what does Will's father start calling him?
    Ⓐ little dolphin
    Ⓑ big shark
    Ⓒ slippery eel
    Ⓓ little fish

68. Kirby says that he saved Will's life. How does he do this?
    Ⓐ Kirby kills a snake just before it bites Will.
    Ⓑ Kirby pulls Will out of the creek after he falls in.
    Ⓒ Kirby teaches Will how to swim, so Will does not drown when he falls in the creek.
    Ⓓ Kirby rescues Will from cattle rustlers who kidnap him along with his father's cattle.

69. Will would probably agree with which statement?
    Ⓐ Learning how to swim is not worth the effort.
    Ⓑ You should never do what older kids say.
    Ⓒ Trying something new can really pay off.
    Ⓓ Learning to ride horses is not worth the effort.

Pretest

Extended-Response Question

21. In "The Creek," Will is nervous at first about learning something new. Explain why he was nervous and describe how he overcame his fears. What did Will learn and how did it help him later on?

_____

_____

_____

_____

_____

_____

_____

_____

_____

_____

_____

_____

End of PART 1: SESSION 3

Note to Students: Your written response will be scored using a rubric like the one on page 54.

PART 2: ISAT for Writing

ISAT for Writing

On the actual ISAT for Writing, you will be given only one thing to write about. You will not have a choice. On this practice test, however, you are given a choice. Be sure to read all three writing topics (the one below and the two on the next page) before you decide what to write about. Once you have chosen a topic, write a paper. You will have forty-five minutes.

Narrative Prompt

Have you ever done something special to help someone? Maybe you raked leaves for an elderly neighbor. Has someone ever done something special to help you? Maybe your mother spent time helping you do a project for school. Think about a time when you helped someone or someone helped you. Write a paper (essay) describing what happened. Explain how it felt to help someone or to have someone help you.

OR

Note to Students: If you respond to the narrative prompt, your written response will be scored using a rubric like the one on pages 55–57.

Pretest

Persuasive Prompt

Think about something in your neighborhood that you would like to change. For example, is there litter on the sidewalks? Do people let their dogs off the leash? Is there a park that needs to be cleaned up? Write a paper (essay) describing what you would like to change in your neighborhood. Also include details about how you could make the change. What you would need to do? Would you need help from friends or adults?

OR

Expository Prompt

Almost everyone has a favorite place. Think about your favorite place. It might be somewhere that you go to feel happy, to have quiet time, or to have fun. Maybe it is a place where something special happened to you. Describe your favorite place. What does it look like? What do you like about it? Why is it your favorite place?

End of PART 2: WRITING

Note to Students: If you respond to the persuasive or expository prompt, your written response will be scored using a rubric like the one on pages 58–60.

Unit 1
Test-Taking Strategies

First Encounter

Read the following story about a gerbil who takes tests. Then answer the questions that follow the story. At the end of the unit, you will be asked to come back to these questions to check your work and fix it if necessary.

Gerbil Genius

by Drew Johnson and Robin Lamb

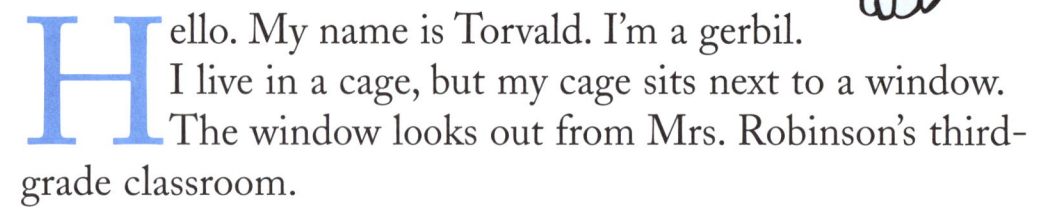

Hello. My name is Torvald. I'm a gerbil. I live in a cage, but my cage sits next to a window. The window looks out from Mrs. Robinson's third-grade classroom.

These days, many people come to see me. My picture has been in the newspaper. I have also been on television. I am a pretty ordinary-looking gerbil. I look like a brown cottonball with whiskers and a tail. However, I am now the most famous gerbil in all of America.

How did I become so famous? Let me tell you. I did it by taking a test. Here's how it happened.

A few weeks ago, Mrs. Robinson started telling her class about the ISAT exams. Students in Illinois take Illinois Standards Achievement Tests (ISATs) in reading, writing, math, social studies, and science. Mrs. Robinson taught her students all about the tests. She explained everything really well. I sat in my cage, ate my carrots and seeds, and listened. I learned a lot.

34 AIM Higher! ISAT Language Arts Review

One day, after school, Mrs. Robinson cleaned out my cage. She usually puts clean paper down in my cage. That day, she was out of clean paper. So, she put some pages of an ISAT practice test in my cage instead.

Then I got lucky. The next day, Billy Thorndike laid a pencil down on top of my cage. The pencil fell through the bars. I chewed the pencil until it was really short. I held it between my teeth. I answered all the questions on the test.

The next week, Mrs. Robinson cleaned out my cage again. That's when she found the pencil and my test with the answers filled in. She could not believe her eyes! Not only had I taken the test. I also got all the answers right!

Mrs. Robinson has the only key to the lock on my cage. So she knew that no one had answered the questions for me. She was really amazed!

Mrs. Robinson put a new test in my cage and gave me back my little pencil. I answered all the questions on the new test, too.

Soon, the whole school was coming to watch me take tests. Then, people came from all over the city. Finally, people from newspapers and television showed up.

I really don't see what the big deal is. After all, tests are not that hard. All you have to do is to learn and practice.

Still, I guess not many gerbils can do what I did. The way I figure it, when someone gives you a test, you can do one of two things.

One: You can tear up the test into little bits and make it into a bed.

Two: You can take the test and do your best on it.

Which would you do? I suggest the second choice. It worked for me! Now I get all the lettuce and seeds I ever wanted, and I am a celebrity…

Whatever that is.

Test-Taking Strategies 35

Your Turn

Exercise A *Answer the following questions. Write your answers in complete sentences.*

1. **A. Remembering Details**

   Where does Torvald's cage sit?

   _____

   B. Thinking about the Details

   Why is Torvald able to hear the lessons about the ISAT tests?

   _____

2. **A. Remembering Details**

   How do the first test and the pencil get into Torvald's cage?

   _____

   B. Thinking about the Details

   How does luck help Torvald?

   _____

3. **A. Remembering Details**

   What does Mrs. Robinson discover when she cleans the cage the second time?

   _____

   B. Thinking about the Details

   Why is Mrs. Robinson so surprised?

   _____
   _____

36 AIM Higher! ISAT Language Arts Review

Exercise B Torvald says that he is now a celebrity. He does not know, however, what a celebrity is. What do you think a celebrity is? Can you give examples of celebrities? Why is Torvald a celebrity? Answer these questions on the lines below.

Meets ISAT
Standards
1.B.1c
2.B.1c
3.A.1
3.C.1a
5.A.1b

1. A *celebrity* is _____
_____.

2. Three examples of celebrities are _____
_____
_____.

3. Torvald is a celebrity because _____
_____
_____
_____
_____
_____
_____
_____.

Test-Taking Strategies

Chapter 1

This Is Only a Test

Taking Tests

You just read a story called "Gerbil Genius." A genius is a very smart person. You can do well on tests without being a genius. Here's how.

> You need to
> - learn how to take tests.
> - practice your reading, writing, and listening skills.
> - practice taking tests.

This book will help you do all these things. It will help make you a great test-taker, just like Torvald!

Throughout your life, you will take many tests. You will take tests in your classes. You will take state tests like the ISAT. You will take tests to get into college. You will take tests to get jobs. Being a good test-taker can make your whole life better.

Understanding Tests

A **classroom test** asks questions about something you have just learned. For example, in science you might learn all about magnets. Then you might take a test on magnets.

The ISAT tests are **general tests.** They test skills you have learned in third grade and before.

Meets ISAT Standards
1.B.1a
1.B.1c

Preparing for Tests

How can you get ready to take these tests? Here are some tips for getting ready for tests, especially tests that cover things you have learned all year:

Getting Ready for Tests

✔ Take notes in class and when you are reading for homework.

✔ Make sure you have a good idea of what will be on the test.

✔ Make a list of everything that you think you will have to know and do for the test.

✔ Study handouts, worksheets, and textbook chapters covered by the test.

✔ Test yourself, or have other people test you.

✔ Use flash cards.

✔ Use your own little tricks to remember things. For example, you can memorize the names of the Great Lakes using the letters in the word **HOMES**: **H**uron, **O**ntario, **M**ichigan, **E**rie, and **S**uperior.

✔ Practice, practice, practice.

✔ Get plenty of rest before the test.

✔ Eat well on the night and morning before the test.

✔ Believe in yourself. Relax. Do not be nervous.

Test-Taking Strategies

Taking Tests

Here's another important tip. After a test, make sure you understand any parts that you got wrong this time. That will help you the next time you have a test!

Tests like the ISAT exams are not like the tests you usually take in your classroom. You cannot just study for them on the night before. That's because they test skills learned over time. The best way to get ready for general tests is to keep practicing your skills. In other words, if you are going to have to take a big test in reading or writing, you should try to read and write regularly.

Try to read a little bit on your own every day. Libraries have lots of good books and magazines for young people. The Internet is also a great place to find interesting reading.

Also, start keeping a journal, just for yourself. A **journal** is a notebook or diary where you write down your ideas, thoughts, and feelings, day by day. You might also write about what happens to you. Write in your journal for a few minutes every day, or at least every other day.

Writing in a Journal

Journals are great for writing practice every day! Here are some ideas for journal writing:

Journal Idea 1: Dear Diary

Just tell what happened in your day.

Journal Idea 2: Feelings First

Tell how you feel about some person, place, thing, or event around you. Also tell why you feel that way.

Journal Idea 3: Daydreams

Let your imagination go wild! Imagine that you are a king or an astronaut or a wild animal. Imagine that you can read other people's minds. Imagine that you are very, very tall or very, very small. Write about whatever you can imagine.

More ▶

Meets ISAT
Standards
1.B.1a
1.B.1c
3.C.1a

Journal Idea 4: News Views

Write down your thoughts about a current event you have learned about from the newspaper, television, or the Internet.

Journal Idea 5: Try It: You'll Like It

Pretend you are writing to a friend. Tell him or her about a video game, television show, book, sports event, audio CD, brand of jeans, or something else that you really liked or disliked.

Journal Idea 6: Things To Do

Make a list of things that you need to do or would like to do someday.

Journal Idea 7: See What You Mean

Describe something. Use words that make it come alive. Describe how it looks, sounds, smells, tastes, and feels.

Journal Idea 8: Snapshots

Describe somebody. You can write about a friend or about someone famous. Tell everything you can about them. Be nice, though!

Whenever you are about to take a general test like the ISAT, you should eat and sleep well before it. In addition, you should try to relax. The big secret to doing well on general skill tests, however, is to practice a little bit on your own, every day. You'll end up a great test-taker, like Torvald!

REMEMBER:

Long before the test, read and write a little bit on your own every day. If you do this, over time, you will build the mental muscles you will need to do well on tests.

Test-Taking Strategies 41

Your Turn

Exercise A Start keeping your own journal. Keep a journal every day for one week (seven days). Begin by putting down the date. Try each one of the types of journal writing described in the chart on pages 40–41.

Exercise B Start a reading log. You can keep the log in a separate part of your journal. In the log, keep track of all the reading that you do on your own, outside of school. For example, your log for three days might look like this:

Monday, September 5	Newspaper Article: "Houseboat Sinks into Lake"
Tuesday, September 6	Internet Article: "King Cobras"
Wednesday, September 7	5 pages of chapter book: The Lion, the Witch, and the Wardrobe

Taking Tests

Test-Taking Tips

So far in this chapter, you have learned some ways to prepare for tests in general. Now, you will learn some tips for answering multiple-choice questions on tests.

Meets ISAT Standards
1.B.1a
1.B.1c
3.C.1a

Multiple-Choice Questions

Many tests are made up of multiple-choice questions. A **multiple-choice question** has two parts: an opening and some answer choices. Only one of the answer choices is the right answer. Your job is to pick the right one.

Sometimes the opening is a question, like this:

1. Who is the main character in "Gerbil Genius"?
   Ⓐ Gerald
   Ⓑ Geraldine
   Ⓒ Mrs. Robinson
   Ⓓ Torvald

Test-Taking Strategies 43

Taking Tests

On some tests you will take, the opening is a sentence that is not finished, like this:

1. The main character in "Gerbil Genius" is
   - Ⓐ Gerald.
   - Ⓑ Geraldine.
   - Ⓒ Mrs. Robinson.
   - Ⓓ Torvald.

Sometimes the opening has a blank to fill in, like this:

1. The character named _____ is a gerbil and a genius.
   - Ⓐ Gerald
   - Ⓑ Geraldine
   - Ⓒ Mrs. Robinson
   - Ⓓ Torvald

Here are some tips for answering multiple-choice questions:

Meets ISAT Standard 1.B.1c

Answering Multiple-Choice Questions

1. If you do not know the answer, go on to the next question. Mark the question you skipped so that you will remember to come back to it later.

2. First, cross out all answers that you are sure are wrong. Then choose the best answer from the possibilities that are left.

3. Pay attention to negative words in openers. **Negative words** are words like **not** and **except.**

4. Sometimes more than one answer will seem right. Choose the best answer.

Suppose you need to answer this question:

1. Who is the main character in "Gerbil Genius"?
   Ⓐ Gerald
   Ⓑ Geraldine
   Ⓒ Mrs. Robinson
   Ⓓ Torvald

You can throw out answers A and B right away. There are no characters in the story named Gerald or Geraldine. That leaves two possible answers: C and D. Then you can ask yourself which of these is the main character. The word *main* means "most important." Mrs. Robinson is not the most important character. The right answer must be D, Torvald.

Test-Taking Strategies   45

Your Turn

Exercise For each of the following questions, draw a line through two answers that are obviously wrong. Then guess the correct answer. Fill in the circle next to that answer.

EXAMPLE: Which of the following people was president of the United States?

- Ⓐ ~~Mickey Mouse~~
- ● John Quincy Adams ← correct
- Ⓒ ~~Superman~~
- Ⓓ Thomas Edison

1. Which of the following people wrote the novel *Charlotte's Web*?
   - Ⓐ Luke Skywalker
   - Ⓑ Michael Jordan
   - Ⓒ E. B. White
   - Ⓓ Kenneth Grahame

2. Which state is found in the midwestern part of the United States?
   - Ⓐ North Carolina
   - Ⓑ Russia
   - Ⓒ Africa
   - Ⓓ Indiana

3. What do gerbils eat?
   - Ⓐ hot dogs
   - Ⓑ seeds
   - Ⓒ ice cream
   - Ⓓ pineapple

4. Marco Polo brought gunpowder back to Europe from
   - Ⓐ China.
   - Ⓑ North America.
   - Ⓒ Mars.
   - Ⓓ Middle Earth.

Taking Tests

Short- and Long-Answer Questions

When you answer a multiple-choice question, the right answer is already there. You just have to figure out which one it is. On some tests, however, you are not given a set of answers to choose from. You have to write your own answers. A test question for which you must write your own answer is called an **extended-response question.**

Here are some extended-response questions:

1. Name the first four presidents of the United States.

2. Write an essay telling what kind of animal makes the best pet and why.

Some extended-response questions have short answers. The answer to Question 1, above, is this:

The first four presidents of the United States were George Washington, John Adams, Thomas Jefferson, and James Madison.

To answer other extended-response questions, you have to create a long answer. Question 2, above, asks the test-taker to create an essay. An **essay** is a piece of writing with several paragraphs about a single part of a larger topic.

Meets ISAT Standards
1.B.1a
1.B.1c
3.C.1a

Test-Taking Strategies 47

Taking Tests

You will learn a lot more about answering extended-response questions later in this book. For now, here are a few tips:

Answering Extended-Response Questions

1. Read the question carefully several times.
2. Decide how long your answer needs to be. Do you need to write a sentence? Several sentences? A paragraph? Several paragraphs?
3. Answer the question completely.
4. If the question has several parts, answer all of the parts.
5. Answer in complete sentences unless you are told otherwise.
6. Begin each sentence with a capital letter and end it with an end mark such as a period or question mark. Use a capital for the first letter of every name and important word in a title and place.
7. Indent each paragraph.
8. Read over your answer carefully when you are finished.
9. Make changes if you need to do so.

Your Turn

Exercise Read each extended-response question below. Then read the answer to each question. On the lines following each answer, tell what is wrong with the answer.

Meets ISAT
Standards
1.B.1a
1.B.1c
3.A.1
3.B.1b
3.C.1a

1. QUESTION: What causes the seasons? Explain, using complete sentences.

    ANSWER: Earth tilted. Part closer to sun has summer. Further away, winter.

2. QUESTION: Name two birds that are related to crows. Tell how they are alike and how they are different.

    ANSWER: Two birds that are related to crows are ravens and bluejays.

3. QUESTION: What are the primary colors?

    ANSWER: Red, yellow, and blue.

More ▶

Test-Taking Strategies 49

Your Turn

Meets ISAT Standards
1.B.1a
1.B.1c
3.A.1
3.B.1b
3.C.1a

4. **QUESTION:** Who were the first four presidents of the United States?

   ANSWER: washington, adams, jefferson, and madison

5. **QUESTION:** Name a country you would like to visit. Tell what you would like to see there.

   ANSWER: I would like to visit China.

Chapter 2

ISAT for Reading
ISAT for Writing

Understanding Your State Tests

Students in the state of Illinois are required to take state tests in reading and writing. The names of these tests are as follows:

- The Illinois Standards Achievement Test for Reading
- The Illinois Standards Achievement Test for Writing

These tests are commonly known as the **ISAT for Reading** and the **ISAT for Writing.** The Pretest and Posttest in this book are like the ISAT reading and writing tests.

Test-Taking Strategies

Understanding Your State Tests

Here's what you can expect on these exams:

ISAT for Reading

The ISAT for Reading has three forty-minute sessions.

In **Session 1,** you will be given fourteen **word-analysis questions.** These will test your ability to use phonics, word patterns, and other word-analysis skills to recognize words. Next, you will be given one passage to read. You will answer fourteen to sixteen **multiple-choice questions** about the passage. Each multiple-choice question gives you four answers to choose from. Only one of the answers is correct.

In **Session 2,** you be given one passage to read. You will answer seventeen to twenty multiple-choice questions about the passage. Then, you will answer, in writing, one extended-response question about the reading. An **extended-response question** asks you to come up with your own fairly long answer. In your answer, you will have to use information from the reading.

Session 3 will be just like Session 2, but the reading passage will be different.

The reading passages will be stories or informational pieces. The stories may be imaginary (fiction) or true (nonfiction). The informational pieces may include articles from magazines or newspapers. The questions on the ISAT for Reading will test your ability to comprehend the reading passages. When you **comprehend** something, that means that you understand it. Chapters 4 through 6 will help teach you to make sense of stories and informational readings.

ISAT for Writing

The ISAT Writing exam has one forty-minute session.

You will be given a single writing prompt. A **writing prompt** is a set of directions for writing. You will spend the entire session writing your response.

Each ISAT Writing exam contains a persuasive, expository, or a narrative writing prompt.

- A **persuasive** writing prompt asks you to take a position and develop one side of an argument.
- An **expository** prompt asks you to give information.
- A **narrative** prompt asks you to do one of two things:
  1. Tell about an important experience. If the prompt asks you to tell about an experience, you are expected to tell the story of the event and describe the reactions of the participants.
  2. Report and record reactions to an observed event. If the prompt asks you to report on an event, you are expected to tell the story of the event and describe the reactions of the participants.

You will not know which type of prompt you will have to respond to until you begin the test. Chapters 9 through 15 of this text are devoted to teaching you writing skills and preparing you for the ISAT Writing exam.

Meets ISAT
Standards
1.A.1a
1.A.1b
1.B.1b
1.B.1c
2.B.1a
2.B.1c
3.C.1a

Look back over the Pretest on pages 1 through 32. Think about what the test looks like and about the types of question on it.

Understanding Your State Tests

Meets ISAT Standards
1.B.1a
1.B.1c
1.C.1b
3.A.1
3.B.1b
3.C.1a

A rubric is a list of criteria, or standards, used to judge a piece of writing. Your written responses on the ISAT for Reading and the ISAT for Writing will be scored using rubrics like the ones that appear below and on the following pages. Study these rubrics. Then, use them to judge the writing that you do for the Pretest and Posttest in this book. This will help you to understand how your written responses on the state tests will be scored. The rubric below is like the one that will be used to score your written responses to the extended-response questions in the ISAT for Reading. A 4 is the highest score.

Extended-Response Reading Rubric*

4
- I explain the main ideas and important information from the text.
- I connect my own ideas or experiences to the author's ideas.
- I use examples and important details to support my answer.
- I balance the author's ideas with my own ideas.

3
- I explain some of the main ideas and important information from the text.
- I connect some of my own ideas or experiences to the author's ideas.
- I use some examples and important details to support my answer.
- I balance only some of the author's ideas with my own ideas.

2
- I explain only a few ideas from the text.
- I summarize the text without including any of my own ideas or experiences.

OR
- I explain my own ideas without explaining the text.
- I use general statements instead of specific details and examples.

1
- I explain little or nothing from the text.
- I use incorrect or unimportant information from the text.
- I write too little to show I understand the text.

0
- I write nothing.
- I do not respond to the task.

*These student-friendly rubrics are available online at the Illinois State Board of Education Web site: http://www.isbe.state.il.us

This rubric is like the one that will be used to score your response to the narrative writing prompt in the ISAT for Writing. On this rubric, a 6 is the highest score.

Rubric for Narrative Writing*

Score: 6

Focus
- I wrote a story on one subject.
- I included reactions to events.
- I wrote a good closing.

Elaboration
- I used specific details to tell about the events and reactions.
- I wrote a lot about the events in the story.
- I used words that made the story more interesting.

Organization
- My story has a beginning, middle, and end.
- My story has paragraphs for each event or main part.
- I used transitions between paragraphs so that the parts of the story fit together smoothly.
- My sentences are interesting, and they fit together.

Integration
- My paper is fully developed and is outstanding in all areas.

Score: 5

Focus
- I wrote a story on one subject.
- I included reactions to events.
- I wrote a closing.

Elaboration
- I used some specific details.
- I wrote a lot about some events in the story.
- I used some interesting words.

Organization
- My story has a beginning, middle, and end.
- My story has paragraphs for most events or main parts.
- Most of the paper is connected with appropriate transitions.

Integration
- My paper has everything it needs, but there is room for improvement.

More ▶

*These student-friendly rubrics are available online at the Illinois State Board of Education Web site: http://www.isbe.state.il.us

Understanding Your State Tests

Narrative Writing Rubric, continued

Score: 4

Focus
- I wrote a story about one subject, but the reader may need to read the prompt to understand what my writing is about.
- I included some reactions to events.
- My story ends suddenly without a closing.

Elaboration
- I used only a few details to tell my story.
  OR
- The details I did include look like a list.

Organization
- My story has a plan, but the plan is not clear.
- My story flows from beginning to middle to end, but there are some gaps in time.
- Not all events or main parts are paragraphed
- I left out some transitions.

Integration
- My paper is simple, but it includes the basics.

Score: 3

Focus
- My subject is clear, but the events in it are confusing.
- I did not tie events together into one story.
- I did not include reactions.
- I did not write enough.
- I may not have written a narrative paper.

Elaboration
- I did not tell enough about my ideas, or the details I did include look like a list.
- I may not have written enough.

Organization
- The plan of my paper is not clear.
- My paper has few transitions that make sense.
- My paper may not have enough writing.

Integration
- My paper is partially developed with some parts not developed fully.

More ▶

Narrative Writing Rubric, continued

Meets ISAT Standards
1.B.1c
3.A.1
3.B.1b
3.C.1a

Score: 2

Focus
- My story is confusing.
- I did not include reactions.
- I did not write enough.
- Events in my story do not go together.

Elaboration
- I tried to use details, but they are unclear.
- I did not write enough.

Organization
- My paper is confusing. It has ideas, but they don't fit together to tell a story.
- I did not write enough.

Integration
- My story is confusing, with big parts missing.

Score: 1

Focus
- My story is told so that it is confusing.
- I did not write enough.

Elaboration
- I did not include any details.
- I did not write enough.

Organization
- My story is very confusing.
- I did not write enough.

Integration
- I did not follow the directions.
- I did not write enough.

Conventions   Score: 2
- I use complete sentences.
- I spell most common words correctly.
- I use capitalization and punctuation correctly.
- I have some major errors, but readers can still understand my writing.

Conventions   Score: 1
- I have many major errors.
- I have so many errors that readers cannot understand my writing.

Test-Taking Strategies 57

Understanding Your State Tests

This rubric is like the one that will be used to score your response to the persuasive or expository writing prompt on the ISAT for Writing. On this rubric, a 6 is the highest score.

Rubric for Persuasive or Expository Writing*

Score: 6

Focus
- I introduced my topic clearly.
- My paper stays on topic all the time, and it makes sense.
- The closing relates to the topic.
- If I previewed, I wrote about each point I mentioned in the preview.

Support
- I used many details and examples to explain my subject or position.
- My word choice is interesting.

Organization
- My paper has a plan.
- Paragraphs are connected, and all the transitions are appropriate.
- All the sentences do not start the same way.

Integration
- My paper is fully developed and is outstanding in all areas.

Score: 5

Focus
- I introduced my subject or position.
- I kept my paper focused at all times, and my ideas make sense.
- If I previewed, I wrote about each point I mentioned in the preview.

Support
- I used some details and examples to explain my subject or position.

Organization
- My paper has a plan.
- My paper is connected between paragraphs, and most transitions are appropriate.
- A few ideas don't fit the plan.

Integration
- My paper has everything it needs, but there is room for improvement.

More ▶

*These student-friendly rubrics are available online at the Illinois State Board of Education Web site: http://www.isbe.state.il.us

58 AIM Higher! ISAT Language Arts Review

Persuasive or Expository Writing Rubric, continued

Meets ISAT Standards
1.B.1c
3.A.1
3.B.1b
3.C.1a

Score: 4

Focus
- The subject may not be clear to the reader.
- The paper sometimes drifts from the subject, and the paper sometimes doesn't make sense.
- There may not be a closing.
- Not every point that was previewed is explained in the paper.

Support
- The paper has few details and few examples as part of the explanation.
- Details may look like a list.

Organization
- My paper has a plan, but it may not be clear to my readers.
- My paper has some connections between paragraphs, but not all of them are appropriate.
- Some ideas don't fit the plan of the paper.

Integration
- My paper is simple, but it includes the basics.

Score: 3

Focus
- The subject is not very clear.
- I wrote about many ideas with more than one subject.
- I may not have written enough.
- My paper may not be persuasive or expository.

Support
- I did not explain my ideas.
- Details are a list.
- I may not have written enough.

Organization
- The plan of my paper is not clear.
- My paper has transitions that do not make sense.
- Many ideas do not fit the plan. I did not write a persuasive or expository paper.
- I may not have written enough.

Integration
- My paper is partially developed with small parts that are not developed completely.

More ▶

Test-Taking Strategies

Understanding Your State Tests

Meets ISAT Standards
1.B.1c
3.A.1
3.B.1b
3.C.1a

Persuasive or Expository Writing Rubric, continued

Score: 2

Focus
- The subject of my paper is not clear.
- Ideas in the paper do not seem to go together.
- I may not have written enough.

Support
- I tried to write details.
- My details may be unclear.
- I may not have written enough.

Organization
- The plan of my paper is confusing.
- I may not have written enough.

Integration
- My ideas are confusing to my readers because big parts are missing.
- I may not have written enough.

Return to the questions you answered at the beginning of this unit. Check your work and fix it if necessary. Give your work to your teacher for grading.

Score: 1

Focus
- The paper has no topic.
- I did not write enough.

Support
- I did not include details.
- I did not write enough.

Organization
- The paper is very confusing.
- I did not write enough.

Integration
- I did not follow the directions.
- I did not write enough.

Conventions   Score: 2
- I used complete sentences.
- I spelled most common words correctly.
- I used capitalization and punctuation correctly.
- I have some major errors, but readers can still understand my writing.

Conventions   Score: 1
- I have many major errors.
- I have so many errors that readers cannot understand my writing.

Unit 2
Reading Skills Review

First Encounter

Read this selection about milk. Then answer the questions that follow the selection. At the end of the unit, you will be asked to return to these questions to check your work and fix it if necessary.

Make Mine Milk

by Betsy Sebold

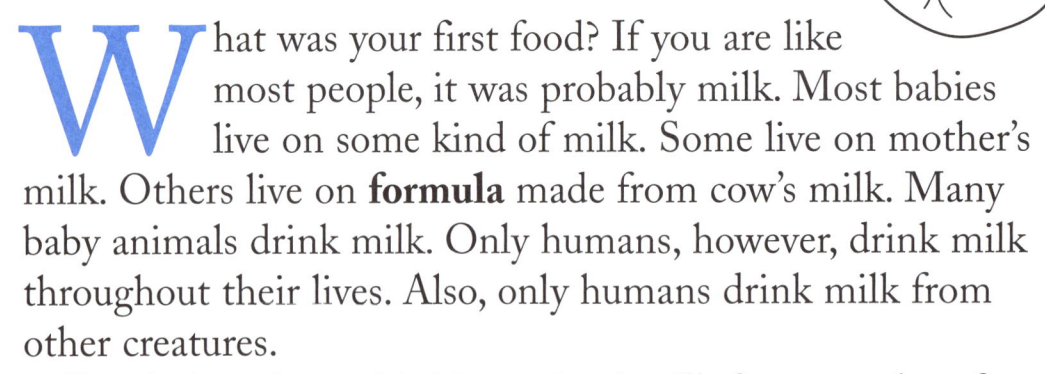

What was your first food? If you are like most people, it was probably milk. Most babies live on some kind of milk. Some live on mother's milk. Others live on **formula** made from cow's milk. Many baby animals drink milk. Only humans, however, drink milk throughout their lives. Also, only humans drink milk from other creatures.

People have been drinking animal milk for more than five thousand years. Around the world, people drink milk from many different animals, including camels, goats, horses, llamas, reindeer, sheep, water buffalo, and yaks. Most of the milk that people drink, however, comes from cows.

Some Common Dairy Products

Butter

Buttermilk

Cheese
(including Blue, Brick, Brie, Cheddar, Colby, Gouda, Limburger, Mozzarella, Parmesan, Provolone, Ricotta, Romano, and Swiss)

Cheese spreads

Cottage cheese

Cream

Cream cheese

Evaporated milk

Ice cream

Malted milk

Milk
(including whole milk, reduced-fat milk, and skim milk)

Powdered milk

Sherbet

Sour cream

Sweetened condensed milk

Yogurt

Dairy Products

Milk from cows is used to make many foods. These foods made from milk are called **dairy products.**

Dairy Cows

In the United States, most dairy cows are **Holsteins.** A Holstein is white with black spots. The spots are different on every Holstein. So, a cow's spots are like fingerprints on a person! Holsteins make lots and lots of milk. A single cow can produce 2,305 gallons of milk a year. That's more than one hundred glasses of milk every day! To make that much milk, a cow must drink enough water every day to fill half a bathtub! Other types of dairy cow include **Guernseys, Jerseys, Brown Swiss,** and **Ayrshires.**

Reading Skills Review

First Encounter

From the Cow to Your Table

When milk comes out of a cow, it is hot. It is 101 degrees Fahrenheit. The milk is quickly cooled to around 40 degrees. Two parts that make up milk are **casein** (milk protein) and **milk fat.** Both are white and give milk its white color.

Milk from a dairy farm is sent to a factory. At the factory, three things happen to the milk. It is pasteurized, homogenized, and fortified.

When milk is **pasteurized,** it is quickly heated and then cooled to kill germs. The germs killed by this process are harmful bacteria. If milk is not pasteurized, the germs in it can make people sick.

When milk is **homogenized,** it is pushed through tiny holes that break the fat in it down into tiny pieces. Homogenizing keeps milk from separating into skim milk and cream.

When milk is **fortified,** Vitamin D is added to it. **Vitamin D** is important. It helps the body to be healthy and to grow.

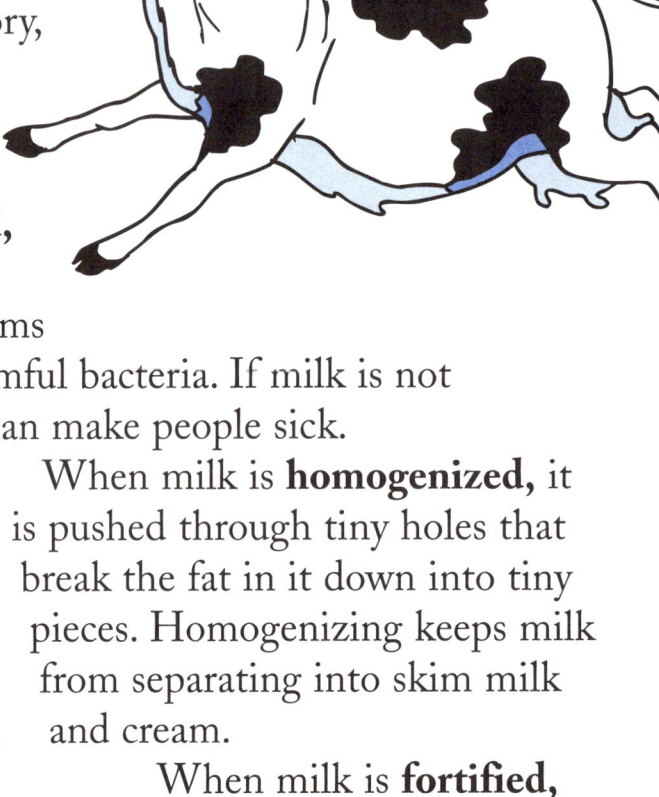

Types of Milk

When you go to the grocery store, you will see different types of milk. This chart describes the differences:

Name	Amount of Milk Fat	Calories (per cup)
Whole milk	3.5 percent	150
Reduced-fat milk	2 percent	122
Low-fat milk	1 percent	102
Skim milk Fat-free milk	less than 0.5 percent	80

Stores also carry buttermilk. **Buttermilk** is made from nonfat or lowfat milk. Tiny creatures called **bacteria** are added to the milk. The bacteria are helpful "germs" in this case. They cause the milk to **curdle,** or become sour and lumpy. Buttermilk is great for cooking. There are also **sweetened, flavored milks,** such as chocolate milk and strawberry milk.

Milk and Health

The U.S. government says that people should drink three glasses of milk or eat three servings of dairy products every day. Milk has lots of **calcium.** Calcium helps to build strong bones and teeth. Milk also has important vitamins.

Some people are allergic to milk. Others are lactose intolerant. This means that their bodies cannot break down the **lactose,** or milk sugar, in milk. These people have to get their calcium and vitamin D from other foods. Green vegetables, such as broccoli and spinach, are good sources of calcium. People who cannot drink milk should eat plenty of these vegetables.

Your Turn

Exercise A Fill in the circle next to the correct answer to each question.

1. Which of the following is NOT a dairy product?
   - Ⓐ spinach
   - Ⓑ mozzarella
   - Ⓒ cottage cheese
   - Ⓓ malted milk

2. What is this article MOSTLY about?
   - Ⓐ how milk is used in cooking
   - Ⓑ healthy eating and exercise
   - Ⓒ where milk comes from and why people drink it
   - Ⓓ what to do if you are allergic to milk

3. What is lactose?
   - Ⓐ milk protein
   - Ⓑ milk fat
   - Ⓒ milk sugar
   - Ⓓ cream from milk

4. Most dairy cows in the United States are
   - Ⓐ Guernseys.
   - Ⓑ Jerseys.
   - Ⓒ Brown Swiss.
   - Ⓓ Holsteins.

5. Which event happens LAST?
   - Ⓐ The milk is pasteurized.
   - Ⓑ The warm milk comes out of the cow.
   - Ⓒ The milk arrives in stores.
   - Ⓓ Vitamins are added.

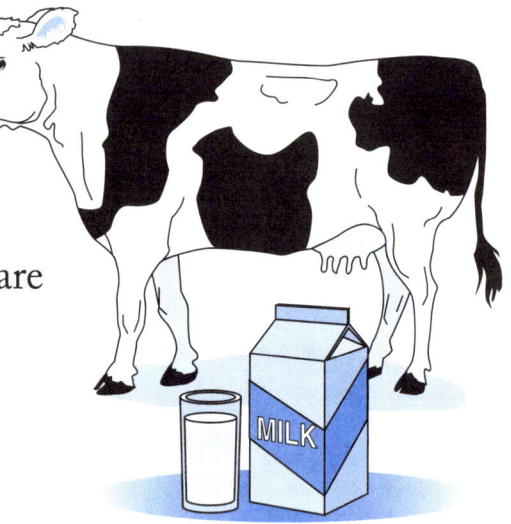

AIM Higher! ISAT Reading and Writing

6. Raw milk that is not pasteurized is more dangerous than pasteurized milk because it

    Ⓐ has lactose, or milk sugar, in it.

    Ⓑ may have harmful germs in it.

    Ⓒ has too much water in it.

    Ⓓ has casein, or milk protein, in it.

7. Milk is white because it has

    Ⓐ casein and milk fat in it.

    Ⓑ bacteria (germs) in it.

    Ⓒ cheese and butter in it.

    Ⓓ water in it.

8. Homogenizing

    Ⓐ adds vitamins to milk.

    Ⓑ keeps cream from separating out of the milk.

    Ⓒ kills harmful bacteria in milk.

    Ⓓ heats milk and then cools it quickly.

9. Reduced-fat milk has

    Ⓐ 3.5 percent milk fat.

    Ⓑ 2 percent milk fat.

    Ⓒ 1 percent milk fat.

    Ⓓ less than 0.5 percent milk fat.

10. Why is it important for people with milk allergies to eat vegetables like broccoli and spinach?

    Ⓐ They are good sources of lactose.

    Ⓑ They are good sources of milk.

    Ⓒ They are good sources of calcium.

    Ⓓ They are good sources of milk fat.

Meets ISAT Standards
1.A.1a
1.A.1b
1.B.1c
1.C.1b
1.C.1d
1.C.1f

Your Turn

Exercise B People need animals. One example of that is the way we depend on dairy cows. Why are dairy cows important to us? Write a paragraph. In your paragraph, tell what dairy cows do for humans. Use facts from the article to support your main idea. Write a draft of your paragraph on your own paper. Check it for errors in spelling, capital letters, and punctuation. Then copy your paragraph onto the lines below.

Chapter 3

Sound Off!

Sounds, Spellings, and Word Parts

Over the past few years, you have learned to read. You learned some words by sight. For example, you probably know these words without sounding them out:

       and   which   her

Some words you learned by sounding them out when reading. When you spell, you sometimes sound out words, too. In this chapter, you will review the sounds and spellings of words. You will also review the parts that make up words. In other words, you will learn how to analyze words. To **analyze** something is to look at all its parts and how they work together. Learning about the parts that make up words will help you to be a better reader. You will also be better prepared to answer the word-analysis questions on the ISAT reading exam.

Meets ISAT Standards
1.A.1a
1.B.1c
3.A.1
3.B.1a
3.B.1b
3.C.1a

Reading Skills Review

Sounds, Spellings, and Word Parts

The Sounds and Spellings of Consonants

Initial, Medial, and Final Consonants

Consonants are sounds like /p/, /m/, /s/, and /j/. Consonants can appear at the beginnings of words, in the middle of words, or at the ends of words.

pig	ha**pp**y	tra**p**
moo	E**mm**y	Pa**m**
sail	ma**ss**ive	me**ss**

Exercise A Look at each picture. Say its name. Write the letter to show where you hear the sound in the name. Is it at the beginning, middle, or the end? Then write the word. The first one has been done for you.

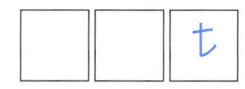

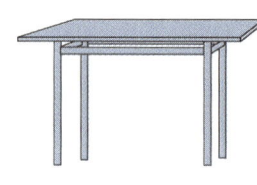

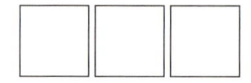

1. **t**

   [_][_][t]   [t][_][_]   [_][t][_]

   hat   table   kitten

2. **m**

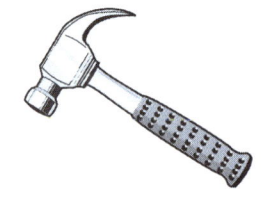

   [_][_][_]   [_][_][_]   [_][_][_]

3. **l**

4. **s**

Exercise B *Follow the directions below.*

1. Write three words that begin with the /p/ sound.
   _____   _____   _____

2. Write three words that end with the /p/ sound.
   _____   _____   _____

3. Write three words with the /p/ sound in the middle.
   _____   _____   _____

Reading Skills Review 71

Sounds, Spellings, and Word Parts

Hard and Soft Consonants

c can sound hard, as in **c**ake or pi**c**nic (/c/ means hard c)

c can sound soft, as in **c**ity, i**c**y, or jui**c**e (/s/ means soft c)

c can sound soft before **e**, **i**, or **y**: **c**ertain, **c**itrus, la**c**y

g can sound hard, as in **g**ood, fo**gg**y, or do**g** (/g/ means hard g)

g can sound soft, as in **g**ym, ca**g**e, or ran**g**er (/j/ means soft g)

g can sound soft before **e**, **i**, or **y** and in the letters **dge**: **g**ee, fra**g**ile, **E**gypt, bri**dge**

Exercise A Circle the letter that stands for the sound of the boldfaced letter or letters in each word.

1. fu**dge**
   /g/ /j/

2. **g**old
   /g/ /j/

3. **g**erbil
   /g/ /j/

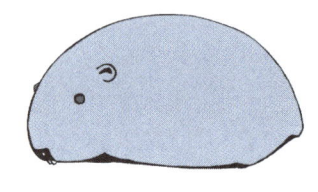

4. **c**yborg
   /k/ /s/

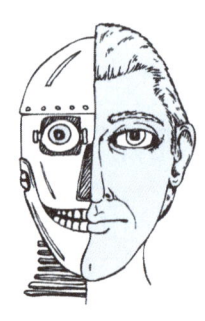

5. **c**one
   /k/ /s/

6. **c**urtain
   /k/ /s/

7.

magic

/g/ /j/

8.

ba**dge**

/g/ /j/

9.

gem

/g/ /j/

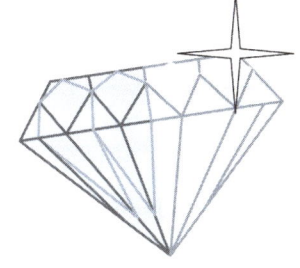

Meets ISAT
Standards
1.A.1a
1.B.1c

10.

curious

/k/ /s/

11.

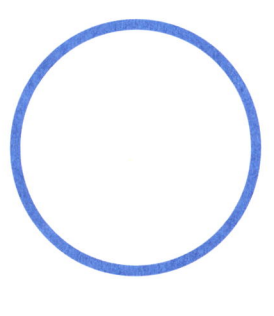

circle

/k/ /s/

12.

bra**c**es

/k/ /s/

Exercise B *Follow the directions below.*

1. Write three words with a soft **c** sound.

   _____   _____   _____

2. Write three words with a soft **g** sound.

   _____   _____   _____

Reading Skills Review 73

Sounds, Spellings, and Word Parts

Consonant Clusters, or Blends

A **consonant cluster,** or **blend,** is two or three consonants used together.

Blends can be made with the letter **r**:
  brake, **cr**ayon, **dr**ink, **fr**eckle, **gr**ape, **pr**ince

Blends can be made with the letter **l**:
  bliss, **cl**ever, **fl**ame, **gl**ide, **pl**anet, **sl**ice

Blends can be made with the letter **s**:
  scarf, **sk**etch, **sm**og, **sn**ow, **sp**ace, **st**orm, **sw**im

Blends can have three letters:
  schooner, **scr**uffy, **shr**imp, **spl**ash, **squ**id, **str**aw, **thr**ead

Some blends come at the ends of words:
  fa**ct**, swi**ft**, qui**lt**, sto**mp**, ba**nd**, ho**nk**, pla**nt**, scri**pt**, de**sk**, bu**rp**, wa**sp**, coa**st**, pu**nch**

Some blends that come at the ends of words are followed by a silent **e**:
  he**dge**, la**nce**, hi**nge**, se**nse**

Exercise For each word, come up with one new blend to make a new word. Write the blend in the blank.

EXAMPLE: de**nse**   de__nt__

1. **bl**imp   ____imp
2. **st**and   sta____
3. wi**sp**   wi____
4. **cr**ow   ____ow
5. **sl**ept   ____ept
6. **dr**ake   ____ake
7. slu**dge**   slu____
8. plu**nge**   plu____
9. **cr**aft   cra____
10. **cl**ock   ____ock

74 AIM Higher! ISAT Reading and Writing

Consonant Digraphs, Consonant Trigraphs, and Silent Consonants

A **digraph** is a single sound spelled with two letters: **ph, sh, th, wh.**

A **trigraph** is a single sound spelled with three letters: **ght, tle.**

Consonant digraphs can appear at the beginnings of some words.
   phone, **sh**ip, **th**ink, **th**en, **wh**eat

Consonant digraphs and trigraphs can appear at the ends of words.
   du**ck**, enou**gh**, ni**ght**, sera**ph**, si**ng**, wi**sh**, wi**th**

Some digraphs and trigraphs have silent letters in them.

co**mb**	(silent **b**)	cha**lk**	(silent **l**)
gnat	(silent **g**)	cas**tle**	(silent **t** and **e**)
ghost	(silent **h**)	**wr**ap	(silent **w**)
knife	(silent **k**)	li**ght**	(silent **gh**)

Meets ISAT Standards
1.A.1a
1.B.1c

Exercise A Draw a box around the digraph. Then write another word that contains the same digraph.

1. thin _____
2. show _____
3. sock _____
4. tough _____

Exercise B Circle the silent letter(s) in each word. If a word has no silent letter(s), cross out the word.

1. climb
2. thistle
3. write
4. bought
5. talk
6. knit
7. lamb
8. though
9. walk
10. often
11. knock
12. would

Reading Skills Review 75

Sounds, Spellings, and Word Parts

The Sounds and Spellings of Vowels

Long and Short Vowels

a, e, i, o, and **u** are **vowels**. Vowels can be long or short.

	a	e	i	o	u
short	mat	pet	sit	not	cut
long	māte	Pēte	sīte	nōte	cūte

In CVC words (consonant + vowel + consonant), the vowel is usually short.
    has, red, pin, fox, luck

In CVCe words (consonant + vowel + consonant + silent **e**), the vowel is usually long.
    face, Steve, five, bone, mule

Exercise A Write the word that names the picture. Then circle the sound of the first vowel. The first one has been done for you.

1. (i) ī

    pig

2. i ī

    _____

3. i ī

    _____

76 AIM Higher! ISAT Reading and Writing

4. a ā   **5.** a ā   **6.** a ā

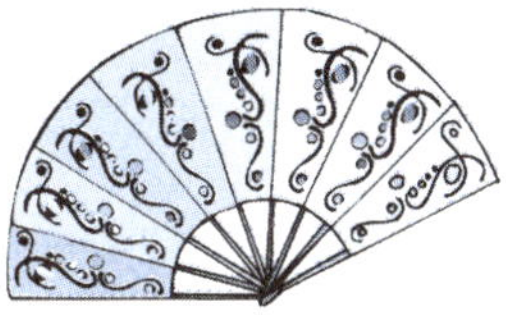

7. u ū   **8.** u ū   **9.** u ū

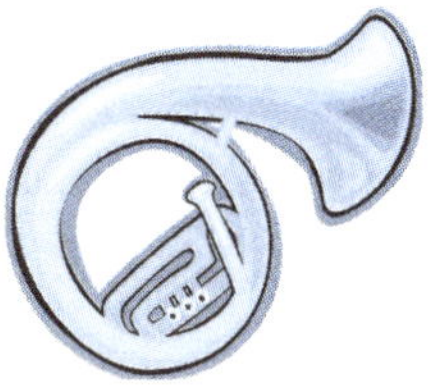

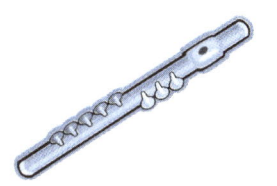

10. o ō   **11.** o ō   **12.** o ō

Exercise B Circle the sound of the first vowel in each word.

1. pet   e ē
2. mete e ē
3. tot   o ō
4. tote o ō
5. cap   a ā
6. cape a ā
7. kit   i ī
8. kite i ī

Reading Skills Review 77

Sounds, Spellings, and Word Parts

Spellings of Long ā, Long ē, and Long ī

Long ā can be spelled **ay**, **ai**, or **eigh**:

    b**ay**   w**ai**t   w**eigh**

Long ē can be spelled **ee** or with a **y** at the end of a word with more than one syllable:

    f**ee**t   sand**y**

Long ī can be spelled with a **y** at the end of a word with more than one syllable:

    b**y**   tr**y**   wh**y**

Exercise Circle the vowel that matches the boldfaced sound in each word.

1. ā ē ī — t**r**ay
2. ā ē ī — fl**y**
3. ā ē ī — gr**ee**t
4. ā ē ī — monk**ey**
5. ā ē ī — funn**y**
6. ā ē ī — pon**y**

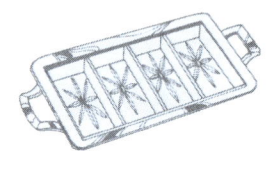

7. ā ē ī

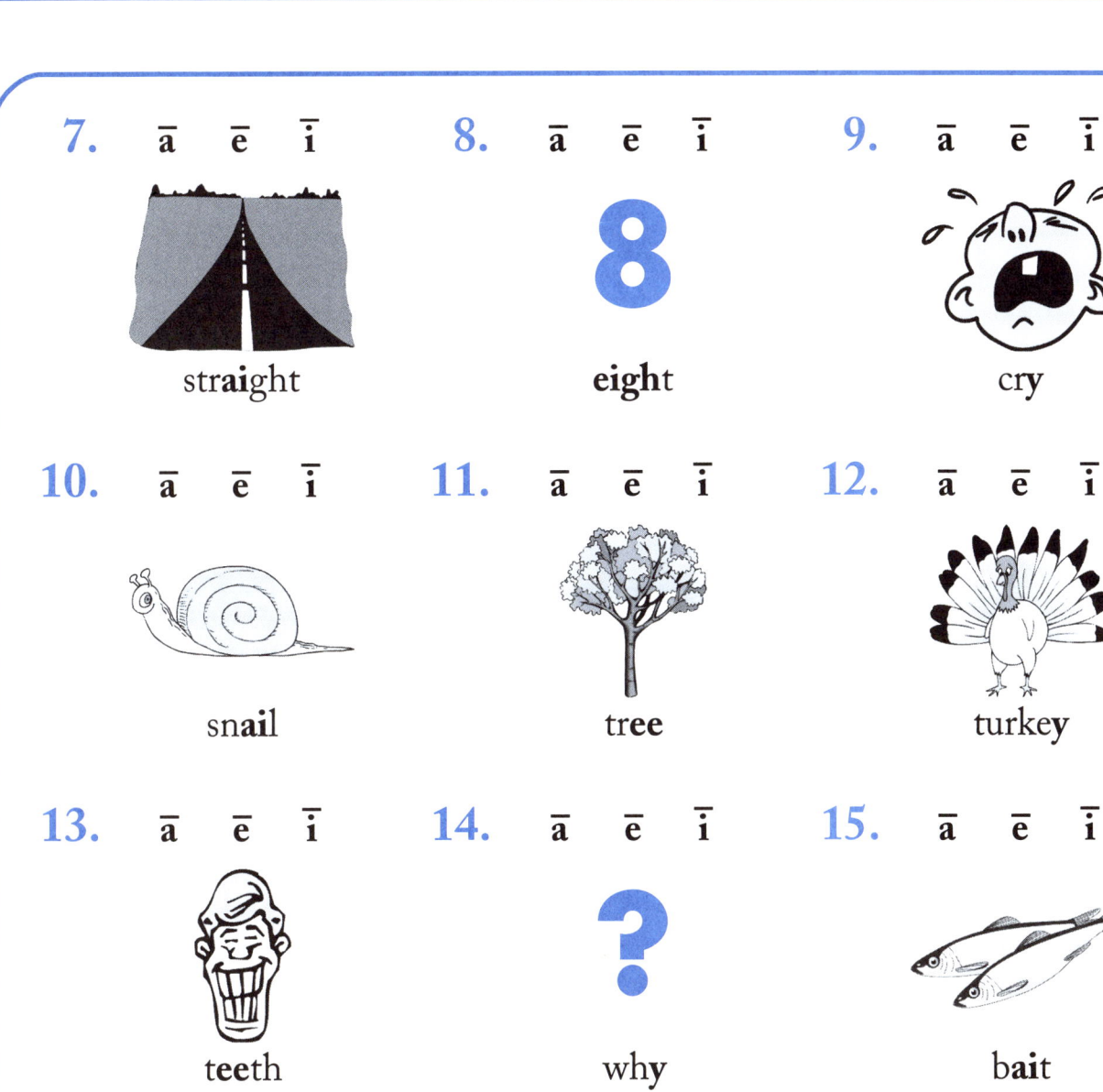

str**ai**ght

8. ā ē ī

eight

9. ā ē ī

cr**y**

Meets ISAT
Standards
1.A.1a
1.B.1c

10. ā ē ī

sn**ai**l

11. ā ē ī

tr**ee**

12. ā ē ī

turk**ey**

13. ā ē ī

t**ee**th

14. ā ē ī

wh**y**

15. ā ē ī

b**ai**t

Reading Skills Review 79

Sounds, Spellings, and Word Parts

Sounds of ei and ie

ei can sound like long **ā**:
  e**i**ght   fr**ei**ght

ei can sound like long **ē**:
  c**ei**ling   rec**ei**pt

ie can sound like long **ī**:
  l**ie**   t**ie**

ie can sound like long **ē**:
  f**ie**ld   ch**ie**f

Exercise Add letters to complete the words in the sentences below. Then circle the vowel sound of the letters you added. Use a dictionary if necessary to check your spellings.

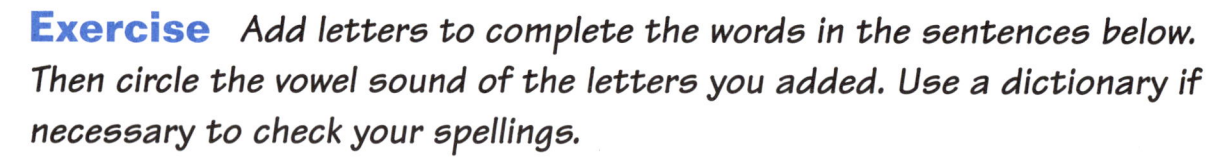

1. Cut me a p____ce of cake.   ā   ē   ī
2. How much do you w____gh?   ā   ē   ī
3. S____ze the day!   ā   ē   ī
4. Make it short. Be br____f.   ā   ē   ī
5. Sandra is my n____ce.   ā   ē   ī
6. This plant has d____d.   ā   ē   ī
7. Have you rec____ved your check?   ā   ē   ī
8. I hear a fr____ght train.   ā   ē   ī
9. Santa drives a sl____gh.   ā   ē   ī
10. Your shoes are unt____d.   ā   ē   ī

Spellings of Long ō

Long ō can be spelled **oe**:

    t**oe**   f**oe**

Long ō can be spelled **oa**:

    t**oa**d   fl**oa**t

Long ō can be spelled with an **o** at the end of a word:

    sol**o**   sopran**o**

Long ō can be spelled with **ow**:

    fl**ow**   r**ow**

The letter **o** followed by **l** and another consonant has the long ō sound:

    tr**oll**   c**old**

Meets ISAT Standards
1.A.1a
1.B.1c

Exercise On the line below each picture, write the word that names what is in the picture. Then circle the word above the picture that spells long ō in the same way. Use a dictionary if necessary to check your spellings.

1. (moat)   tow

    road

2. coast   bowl

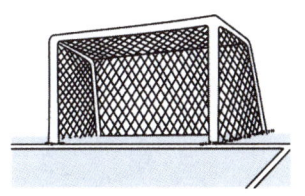

    _____

3. sold   soak

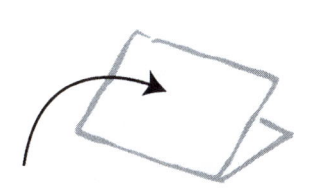

    _____

More ▶

Sounds, Spellings, and Word Parts

4. low   also

5. coal   grow

6. show   hello

7. roll   toast

8. molt   mow

9. hoe   load

10. boast   Joe

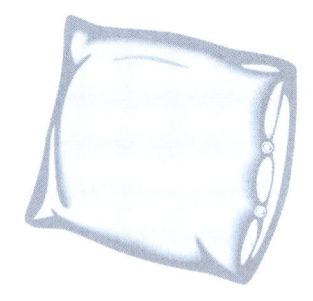

11. roe   foam

12. throw   no

82 AIM Higher! ISAT Reading and Writing

The Vowel Sound /ô/

The sound /ô/ can be spelled in many ways.

o	as in	s**o**ft
a before **l, ll, lk,** or **lt**	as in	**all, talk, Walt**
aw	as in	y**aw**n
au	as in	c**au**ght
ou	as in	**ou**ght

Meets ISAT
Standards
1.A.1a
1.B.1c

Exercise A Write the word with the /ô/ sound that names each picture. Use a dictionary if necessary to check your spellings.

1.

2.

3.

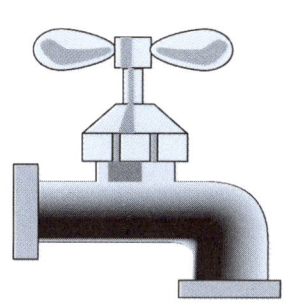

4.

5.

6.

More ▶

Reading Skills Review 83

Sounds, Spellings, and Word Parts

Exercise B Look at each word below. Say the word to yourself. If the word has the /ô/ sound, circle the letters with that sound. If the word does not have the /ô/ sound, draw a line through the word.

EXAMPLES: cl(aw)   ~~pop~~

1. law
2. float
3. flaw
4. auto
5. hot
6. walk
7. sauce
8. call
9. sausage
10. chalk
11. bought
12. cold

Exercise C Circle the word in each pair that has the /ô/ sound.

1. malt   molt
2. flaw   flat
3. bought   book
4. loft   lot
5. bat   balk
6. fat   fawn

84 AIM Higher! ISAT Reading and Writing

Two Sounds of oo

oo can sound like the vowel in **took**.

oo can sound like the vowel in **toot**.

The **oo** sound in **toot** can be spelled in several ways.

oo	as in	ball**oo**n
ue	as in	d**ue**
u_e	as in	fl**u**t**e**
oe	as in	sh**oe**
o	as in	d**o**
ew	as in	fl**ew**
ou	as in	s**ou**p
ui	as in	fr**ui**t

Meets ISAT Standards
1.A.1a
1.B.1c

Exercise A Circle the word that has the same vowel sound as the word in blue that names the picture.

1.

moon

took   toot

2.

woods

took   toot

3.

spoon

took   toot

More ▶

Reading Skills Review   **85**

Sounds, Spellings, and Word Parts

4.

wool

took   toot

5.

noodles

took   toot

6.

poodle

took   toot

Exercise B Look at each word below. Say the word to yourself. If the word has the same vowel sound as the oo in balloon, circle the letters that make the sound. Otherwise, cross out the word.

EXAMPLES: tr(ue)   ~~good~~

1. lute
2. too
3. troupe
4. glue
5. doe
6. shut
7. hound
8. stew
9. to
10. crew
11. chute
12. fuse

86 AIM Higher! ISAT Reading and Writing

The Diphthong /oi/

The sound /oi/ can be spelled **oi** as in b**oi**l or **oy** as in b**oy**.

Meets ISAT Standards
1.A.1a
1.B.1c

Exercise Complete the crossword puzzle using words spelled with oi or oy. Use a dictionary as necessary.

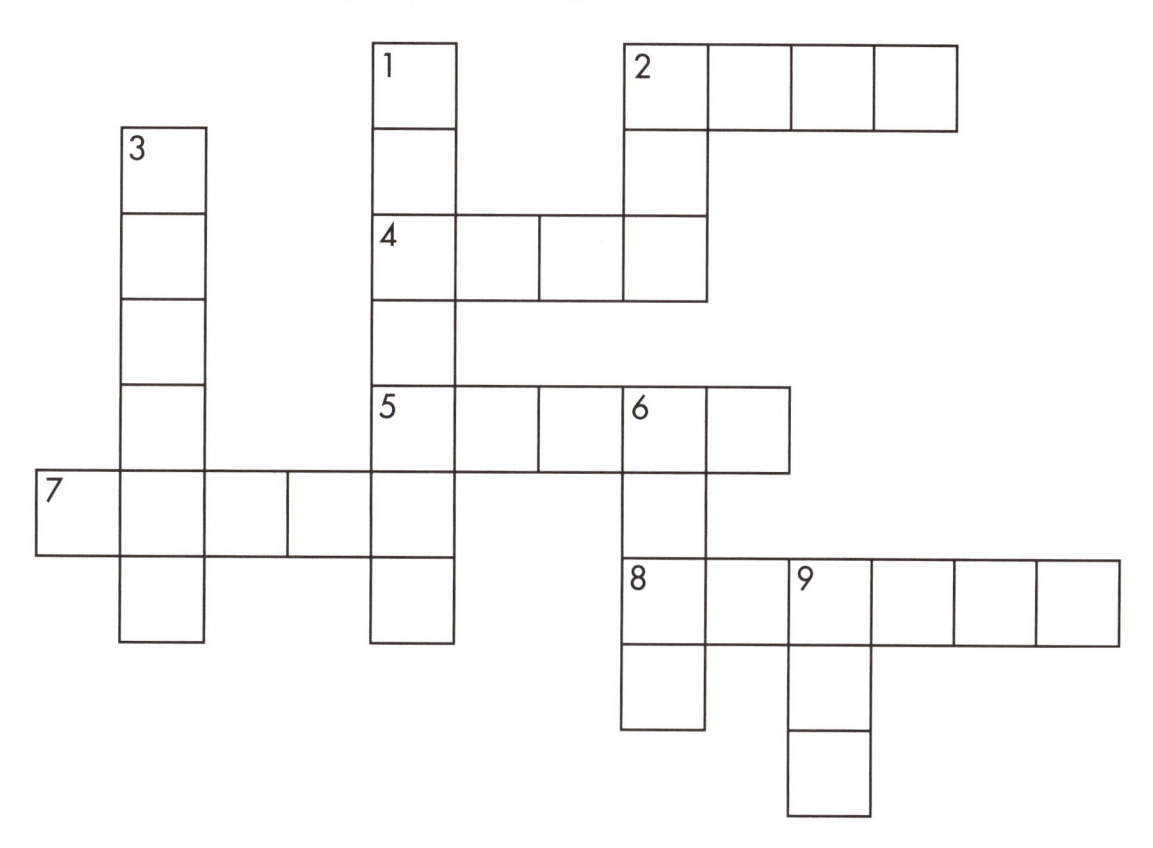

Across

2. cook in hot water
4. greasy
5. faithful
7. what a jackhammer makes
8. shellfish that makes pearls

Down

1. rotten, gone bad
2. male child
3. hire
6. sailor's hello
9. Japanese sauce

Reading Skills Review 87

Sounds, Spellings, and Word Parts

The Two Sounds of ow

ow can have two different sounds, as in gr**ow**l, and as in gr**ow**.

Exercise Fill in the missing letters to make a synonym, or word with the same meaning, as the first group of words. Then circle the *gr* word with the same vowel sound. The first one has been done for you.

			Sounds Like	
EXAMPLE: small city	_t_ ow _n_	(growl)	grow
1. large audience	__ __ ow __	growl	grow
2. turn the soil	__ __ ow	growl	grow
3. pull or carry	__ ow	growl	grow
4. king's headpiece	__ __ ow __	growl	grow
5. a black bird	__ __ ow	growl	grow
6. a weeping tree	__ __ __ __ __ ow	growl	grow
7. wolf's call	__ ow __	growl	grow
8. not a consonant	__ ow __ __	growl	grow
9. run freely (as in water)	__ __ ow	growl	grow
10. cut (as in grass)	__ ow	growl	grow

The Many Sounds of ou

The two letters **ou** can spell many different sounds.

loud

double

group

would

though

cough

Meets ISAT Standards
1.A.1a
1.B.1c

Exercise Circle the two words with the same vowel sound.

1. could through should
2. soup troupe mound
3. ounce trouble bounce
4. scout double touch
5. young dough country
6. county soul trout
7. touch boulder molt
8. poultry bough shoulder
9. souvenir youth couple
10. cougar ouch out

Reading Skills Review 89

Sounds, Spellings, and Word Parts

The Schwa Sound

The schwa sound /ə/ can be spelled with all the vowels in English.

a	as in	afr**a**id
e	as in	nick**e**l
i	as in	div**i**de
o	as in	apr**o**n
u	as in	medi**u**m
y	as in	s**y**ringe

The schwa + **r** sound /ər/ is spelled with **er, ir, ur,** and sometimes, **or** after **w** as in

play**er**	b**ir**th
t**ur**tle	w**or**k

Exercise A Circle the schwa sound in the following words.

1. agree
2. decimal
3. harmony
4. pilgrim
5. giant
6. hydrant
7. chicken
8. camel
9. family
10. upon
11. gallop
12. salad

Exercise B Complete the crossword with words that have the schwa + r sound /ər/. Use a dictionary as necessary to check spellings. One of these has been done for you.

Meets ISAT Standards
1.A.1a
1.B.1c

2. c u r r e n c y

Across

2. paper money
5. storage jar
6. male sibling
7. opposite of last
8. sure
9. wood-eating insect

Down

1. cat's happy sound
2. drape (window covering)
3. back up
4. bend in the road
6. boy's name (short for Albert)
7. solid

Reading Skills Review 91

Sounds, Spellings, and Word Parts

The Parts of Words

Syllables

Words can be divided into syllables. There are as many **syllables** in a word as there are vowel sounds.

one-syllable words: lock, prom, straight, try

two-syllable words: apple, cricket, inside, pretzel

three-syllable words: banana, curious, marshmallow, poisonous

four-syllable words: adorable, escalator, hysterical, tarantula

five-syllable words: characteristic, impenetrable, recreational, understandable

To find out how a word is divided into syllables, check a dictionary.

a•dor•a•ble   char•ac•ter•is•tic

Prefixes, Suffixes, and Base Words

A **base word** is a complete word to which other word parts can be added. *Joy* can be a base word.

joy + *ride* = *joy ride*

en + *joy* = *enjoy*

joy + *ful* = *joyful*

en + *joy* + *ment* = *enjoyment*

A word part added to the beginnings of words is called a **prefix.** Here are some common prefixes:

Meets ISAT
Standards
1.A.1a
1.B.1c

Common Prefixes

Prefix	Meaning	Example
anti–	against	antibacterial (against bacteria)
astro–	star	astronaut (someone who travels among the stars)
auto–	self	autobiography (biography of one's self)
bi–	two	bicycle (two-wheeled vehicle)
co–	with	co-worker (person with whom one works)
extra–, ex–	from, out past	extraterrestrial (from outside Earth) ex-president (past president)
fore–	before, in front of	foretell (predict, or tell beforehand)
hyper–	over, beyond	hyperactive (overly active)
im–, in–	not, opposite of	infrequent (not frequent) impossible (not possible)
mal–	bad	malnutrition (bad or not enough nutrition)

More ▶

Reading Skills Review

Sounds, Spellings, and Word Parts

Prefix	Meaning	Example
micro–	small	*micro*scope (device for looking at small objects)
non–	not, opposite of	*non*combatant (one who does not fight)
over–	too much, extra	*over*load (put on too much weight; excess load)
pre–	before, in front of	*pre*war (before the war)
re–	again, back	*re*play (play again)
semi–	part, half	*semi*circle (half of a circle)
sub–	under, below	*sub*marine (below the sea)
trans–	across, over, change	*trans*continental (across the continent) *trans*form (change from one form to another)
tri–	three	*tri*state (across three states)
un–	not, opposite of	*un*hinge (change or remove a piece of something so that it is not hinged)
uni–	one	*uni*cycle (one-wheeled vehicle)

A word part added to the ends of words is called a **suffix**. Here are some common suffixes:

Common Suffixes

Suffix	Meaning	Example
–able, –ible	capable of, able to	work*able* (capable of working)
–al	of, like	magic*al* (like magic)
–ed	past tense	laugh*ed* (laughing that took place in the past)
–ess	female	lion*ess* (female lion)
–fold	multiplied by	ten*fold* (multiplied by ten)
–ful, full	full of	soul*ful* (full of soul)
–ic	like, similar to, having to do with	angel*ic* (like an angel)
–ily	like	happ*ily* (like someone who is happy)
–ish	like	child*ish* (like a child)
–ism	practice, doctrine, act, or theory of	terror*ism* (act of spreading terror) commun*ism* (Communist doctrine)
–less	without	fear*less* (without fear)
–like	like or similar to	lady*like* (like or similar to a lady)
–ly	in the manner of	calm*ly* (in a calm manner)
–s, –es	plural	game*s*, dish*es* (more than one game, dish)
–ward	in direction of	west*ward* (in a western direction)
–y	full of, containing	fault*y* (containing one or more faults)

More ▶

Meets ISAT Standards
1.A.1a
1.B.1c

Reading Skills Review

Sounds, Spellings, and Word Parts

Suffixes That Form Nouns

Suffix	Meaning	Example
-er, -or	one who	work*er* (one who works)
-ing	thing resulting from an action	paint*ing* (what results when one paints)
-ion, -sion, -tion	act of, state of, thing resulting from	perfec*tion* (state of being perfect)
-ment	act of, state of, thing resulting from	merri*ment* (state of being merry)
-ness	act of, state of, thing resulting from	happi*ness* (state of being happy)

Suffixes Used for Comparisons

Suffix	Meaning	Example
-er	to compare two items	long*er* (as in "A yard is longer than a foot.)
-est	to compare more than two items	fast*est* (as in "Light is the fastest thing in the universe.")

A **root** is a main word part that cannot stand on its own but can be used with other word parts to make new words. Here are some common roots:

Meets ISAT Standards
1.A.1a
1.B.1c

Common Roots

Root	Meaning	Example
auto	self	*auto*matic, *auto*biography
cred, creed	know	in*cred*ible, *cred*ible
log, logy	study	bio*logy*, psycho*logy*
spec	see	in*spect*, *spect*acles
tele	far	*tele*phone, *tele*vision

Exercise A Circle the number that tells how many syllables each word has.

1. mosquito   1 2 3 4 5
2. pepperoni   1 2 3 4 5
3. dessert   1 2 3 4 5
4. environmental   1 2 3 4 5
5. through   1 2 3 4 5

More ▶

Reading Skills Review   97

Sounds, Spellings, and Word Parts

Exercise B Add prefixes or suffixes to create words that have the meaning given in parentheses. Use the charts on pages 93–96.

1. _____-American (against America)
2. south_____ (in a southern direction)
3. excit_____ (capable of being excited)
4. _____transfer_____ (not capable of being transferred, or given by one person to another)
5. _____cycle (vehicle with three wheels)
6. _____function (bad functioning, or not working properly)
7. home_____ (without a home)
8. wasp_____ (like or similar to a wasp)
9. _____public (part public)
10. _____truth_____ (not full of truth)

Exercise C Use a dictionary to find two words with each of the following roots.

1. *auto* _____ _____
2. *cred, creed* _____ _____
3. *log, logy* _____ _____
4. *spec* _____ _____
5. *tele* _____ _____

AIM Higher! ISAT Reading and Writing

Chapter 4

Talking Back to Books

Active Reading

What does it mean to be active? An active person is not a couch potato. He or she does not just sit around. An active person does a lot. For example, an active person might work and jog and bicycle and snowboard. An active person keeps moving.

In addition to having an active body, a person can have an active mind. A person with an active mind thinks a lot. He or she looks at the world carefully, notices details, asks questions, makes connections, dreams, and imagines.

Keeping your body active will make you stronger physically. Keeping your mind active will make you stronger mentally. The secret to becoming a good reader is this:

Have an active mind while you are reading.

Meets ISAT
Standards
1.A.1a
1.B.1a
1.B.1c
5.A.1b

Reading Skills Review

Active Reading

Reading Actively

What, exactly, is reading actively? An **active reader** thinks about what he or she is reading. When you read, you run your eyes across a page. You look at the words and phrases. You may "hear" them inside your head. That's a good start, but the best readers do even more. The best readers are actively involved in what they are reading as soon as they start to read something. They keep thinking about the reading and asking themselves questions about it, even after they are done.

The Process of Active Reading

Before reading: Preview the reading. Look it over. Notice the parts. Think about what you already know about the subject. Think of questions that might be answered by the reading.

During reading: Think about what you are reading. Stay focused. Ask questions. Picture things in your mind. Guess what will happen. Summarize. Make connections. Take notes.

After reading: Sum up what you have read. Try to answer the questions you asked beforehand and as you read the story. Talk about the reading with others. Write about it. Judge the reading: Did you like it? Do you agree with what the writer said?

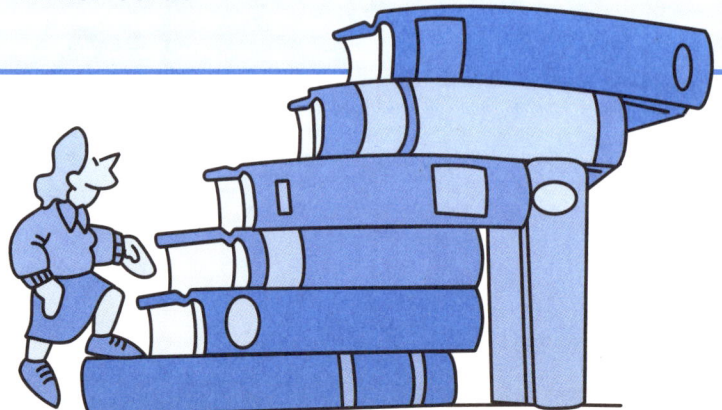

Before Reading

In school and in life, you will read many kinds of writing. You will read stories and poems. You will read magazine articles. You will read short pieces as well as longer books. Any piece of writing that you read is called a **text.**

Whenever you read a text, begin by **previewing** it. First, scan the piece. When you **scan,** you run your eyes quickly over a piece to get an idea of its parts. While you scan the piece, ask yourself two questions:

- What is this piece about?
- What are its parts?

Here are some of the parts that you might see as you scan:

Meets ISAT Standards
1.B.1a
1.B.1c
1.C.1a

Parts of a Text

Title	This is usually at the beginning or top of the first page. The title is the name of the piece of writing. It often gives you an idea of what the piece is about.
Author	This is the person (or persons) who wrote the piece.
Introduction	This is the beginning of the piece. In a fairy tale, the introduction often begins with "Once upon a time...."
Headings, or Subheads	These are little titles that label the parts within a text.
Illustrations	These are pictures, drawings, or maps.
Captions	These are words that explain the illustrations or photos.
Key Words	These are important words in the piece. They might appear in different type. Key words might be in ALL CAPITALS, in **boldface,** in *italics,* or in colored type. They might be underlined.

Reading Skills Review

Your Turn

Exercise A Do NOT read the following text. Instead, scan it, or look over its parts quickly. Circle and label one example of each of the following parts:

Title   Caption
Author   Illustration
Heading   Key word

The first one has been done for you.

Art Smart ← Title
by Kim Tang

What Is Art?

How is a tree different from a painting of a tree? The biggest difference is that a real tree is made by nature. A painting of a tree is made by a person. **Art** is anything beautiful or interesting that is made by people, not by nature. There are many different kinds of art. Together, these are called **the arts.**

Types of Art

In some arts, the artist produces a solid object with three dimensions—height, width, and depth. **Sculpture** is the art in which people make figures out of materials such as wood, metal, or stone. **Ceramics** is the art in which people mold clay into objects such as pots, cups, and figures of people or animals. The clay may be colored with special paints called glazes. Then the pot or object is heated to make it hard. **Architecture** is the art in which people plan and build homes, offices, and other buildings. (A **museum** is a special building for keeping and showing works of art.)

102 AIM Higher! ISAT Language Arts Review

Other artists produce pictures. A picture is usually flat, but it often shows solid things that have three dimensions in real life. **Painting** is a graphic art that involves creating pictures with oils, acrylics, or other types of paint. **Drawing** and **illustrating** involve creating pictures with pencils, pens, chalk, air brushes, and other tools. **Photography** uses a camera to capture pictures on film and paper or in a form you can see on a computer. **Graphic design** uses colors, sizes, and shapes to combine words and pictures in an interesting way in books, magazines, and posters. **Graphic artists** try to make words look more appealing to read on menus or anything else that is printed.

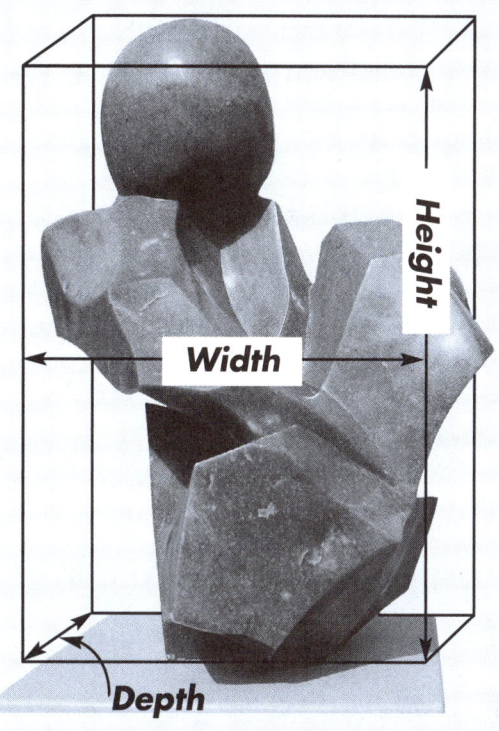

Three-dimensional objects are ones with height, width, and depth.

In the **performance arts,** actors, musicians, or dancers perform in front of other people. **Theater,** or drama, involves actors and, often, costumes, stage sets, and scenery. **Music** involves singing or playing an instrument. **Dance** involves movements of the body. Types of dance include ballet, jazz, modern, and tap.

More ▶

Reading Skills Review 103

Your Turn

Some writers produce literary art. **Writing** is, of course, the act of putting words down on paper. Writing is sometimes done for completely practical purposes. For example, your parents might use writing to create a note for your teacher. However, writing can also be used to create literary art. Stories, poems, and plays are all examples of writing as art.

Does Art Have a Purpose?

Why do people create art? What good is it? What would happen if the arts disappeared entirely tomorrow? These are interesting and important questions.

There is no single reason why people create art. Some people do it just for fun. Some do it because there is something that they really want to say to others. Some do it for money or for fame.

If the arts disappeared tomorrow, people would really miss them. The arts keep us entertained. They also teach us about life and about people, including ourselves. Certainly, the world would be a dull place if all the stories, pictures, music, and dancing disappeared. The arts make life a lot more interesting and a lot more fun.

Exercise B Scan the article on art once more. Do NOT read it carefully, but glance at all the parts. After you have scanned it again, answer these questions. Do not look back at the article.

Meets ISAT Standards
1.B.1c
1.C.1a
1.C.1b

1. What is this article MOSTLY about?

   _____

   _____

2. What do you think you might learn by reading the article?

   _____

   _____

   _____

   _____

Reading Skills Review

Active Reading

Previewing is also called **prereading.** As you scan the text, you look for its parts, such as the title, headings, and key words. In addition, you should think about what you already know about the subject. Anything that you already know about a subject is called your **prior knowledge.** For example, after looking over the piece on art, you might ask yourself a question like this:

> "Hmm. What do I already know about art? When we do art in school, we draw and paint and make models and posters. Maybe art is making things. I know that museums are places where people go to look at art."

Finally, before you read the text carefully, think about what questions it might answer. Here are some questions that one student came up with when previewing "Art Smart":

- What is art?
- What types of art are there?
- What purpose does art have?

Steps in Previewing

- Look over the piece quickly. In other words, scan it. Notice the parts: the title, author, headings, introduction, illustrations, captions, key words, and conclusion.
- Think about what you already know about the subject.
- Come up with some questions that you think the text will answer.

During Reading

As you read, use active reading strategies. **Active reading strategies** are ways to think about what you are reading.

Meets ISAT Standards
1.B.1a
1.B.1c
1.C.1a
1.C.1b
1.C.1d
2.B.1a

Active Reading Strategies

Ask Questions — Ask yourself questions about the text. Then, as you read on, look for answers to your questions.

Visualize — When you **visualize,** you picture things in your mind. The words you read might also appeal to your other senses. Do they make you think of feeling, hearing, tasting, or smelling something? Use your imagination to make what you are reading come alive.

Predict — When you **predict,** you make a guess about something in the future. If you are reading a story, try to guess what will happen next. If what you are reading is not a story, try to predict what the writer will talk about next.

Summarize — When you **summarize,** you tell in a few words what something you heard or read was about.

Make Connections — When you **make connections,** you think about how what you are reading relates to your own experiences. You also think about how it relates to the rest of the world.

Reading Skills Review 107

Active Reading

Here is an example of how one student used active reading strategies while reading "Art Smart":

One Student's Process

Art Smart
by Kim Tang

What Is Art?

How is a tree different from a painting of a tree? The biggest difference is that a real tree is made by nature. A painting of a tree is made by a person. **Art** is anything beautiful or interesting that is made by people, not by nature. There are many different kinds of art. Together, these are called **the arts.**

Types of Art

In some arts, the artist produces a solid object with three dimensions—height, width, and depth. **Sculpture** is the art in which people make figures out of materials such as wood, metal, or stone. **Ceramics** is the art in which people mold clay into objects such as pots, cups, and figures of people or animals. The clay

More ▶

Questioning: Will this piece define what art is?

Visualizing: I see in my mind a drawing of a tree in crayon.

Predicting: I think that the rest of this piece will tell about different kinds of art.

Visualizing: I can picture the Statue of Liberty. It is a solid figure of a lady holding a torch.

108 AIM Higher! ISAT Language Arts Review

may be colored with special paints called **glazes**. Then the pot or object is heated to make it hard. **Architecture** is the art in which people plan and build homes, offices, and other buildings. (A **museum** is a special building for keeping and showing works of art.)

Other artists produce pictures. A picture is usually flat, but it often shows solid things that have three dimensions in real life. **Painting** is a graphic art that involves creating pictures with oils, acrylics, or other types of paint. **Drawing** and **illustrating** involve creating pictures with pencils, pens, chalk, air brushes, and other tools. **Photography** uses a camera to capture pictures on film and paper or in a form you can see on a computer. **Graphic design** uses colors, sizes, and shapes to combine words and pictures in an interesting way in books, magazines, and posters. **Graphic artists** try to make words look more appealing to

More ▶

Meets ISAT
Standards
1.B.1a
1.B.1c
1.C.1a
1.C.1b
1.C.1d
2.B.1a

Summarizing: So, people who do sculpture, ceramics, and architecture produce solid, three-dimensional works of art.

Making Connections: I remember using poster paints to make pictures in class.

Questioning: So, is an advertisement in a magazine an example of graphic design? How about a label on a box in a grocery store?

Reading Skills Review

Active Reading

read on menus or anything else that is printed.

In the **performance arts,** actors, musicians, or dancers perform in front of other people. **Theater,** or drama, involves actors and, often, costumes, stage sets, and scenery. **Music** involves singing or playing an instrument. **Dance** involves movements of the body. Types of dance include ballet, jazz, modern, and tap.

Some writers produce literary art. **Writing** is, of course, the act of putting words down on paper. Writing is sometimes done for completely practical purposes. For example, your parents might use writing to create a note for your teacher. However, writing can also be used to create literary art. Stories, poems, and plays are all examples of writing as art.

More ▶

Making Connections: Dancing is my favorite art. I love dancing!

Making Connections: So, when we do writing in school, are we really learning how to create art? Wait a minute. Not all writing is art. I think something has to be interesting or beautiful to be art.

Does Art Have a Purpose?

Why do people create art? What good is it? What would happen if the arts disappeared entirely tomorrow? These are interesting and important questions.

There is no single reason why people create art. Some people do it just for fun. Some do it because there is something that they really want to say to others. Some do it for money or for fame.

If the arts disappeared tomorrow, people would really miss them. The arts keep us entertained. They also teach us about life and about people, including ourselves. Certainly, the world would be a dull place if all the stories, pictures, music, and dancing disappeared. The arts make life a lot more interesting and a lot more fun.

Making Connections: Why do I like to dance? Because it feels good. That's one reason to do art.

Meets ISAT Standards
1.B.1a
1.B.1c
1.C.1a
1.C.1b
1.C.1d
2.B.1a

Making Connections: I have read about governments that outlawed music and art. That would be terrible!

Summarizing: So, art is fun and people learn from it. Those are the main reasons for it.

Reading Skills Review 111

Your Turn

Exercise Here is the same article about milk that you read at the beginning of this unit. As you read it again, make notes on the lines to the right. Be an active reader. Ask questions. Visualize. Predict. Summarize. Make connections.

Make Mine Milk
by Betsy Sebold

What was your first food? If you are like most people, it was probably milk. Most babies live on some kind of milk. Some live on mother's milk. Others live on **formula** made from cow's milk. Many baby animals drink milk. Only humans, however, drink milk throughout their lives. Also, only humans drink milk from other creatures.

People have been drinking animal milk for more than five thousand years. Around the world, people drink milk from many different animals, including camels, goats, horses, llamas, reindeer, sheep, water buffalo, and yaks. Most of the milk that people drink, however, comes from cows.

Dairy Products

Milk from cows is used to make many foods. These foods made from milk are called **dairy products.**

More ▶

Meets ISAT
Standards
1.B.1a
1.B.1c
1.C.1a
1.C.1b
1.C.1d
2.B.1a

Some Common Dairy Products

Butter

Buttermilk

Cheese
  (including Blue, Brick, Brie, Cheddar, Colby, Gouda, Limburger, Mozzarella, Parmesan, Provolone, Ricotta, Romano, and Swiss)

Cheese spreads

Cottage cheese

Cream

Cream cheese

Evaporated milk

Ice cream

Malted milk

Milk
  (including whole milk, reduced-fat milk, and skim milk)

Powdered milk

Sherbet

Sour cream

Sweetened condensed milk

Yogurt

More ▶

Reading Skills Review

Your Turn

Dairy Cows

In the United States, most dairy cows are **Holsteins.** A Holstein is white with black spots. The spots are different on every Holstein. So, a cow's spots are like fingerprints on a person! Holsteins make lots and lots of milk. A single cow can produce 2,305 gallons of milk a year. That's more than one hundred glasses of milk every day! To make that much milk, a cow must drink enough water every day to fill half a bathtub! Other types of dairy cow include **Guernseys, Jerseys, Brown Swiss,** and **Ayrshires.**

More ▶

From the Cow to Your Table

When milk comes out of a cow, it is hot. It is 101 degrees Fahrenheit. The milk is quickly cooled to around 40 degrees. Two parts that make up milk are **casein** (milk protein) and **milk fat.** Both are white and give milk its white color.

Milk from a dairy farm is sent to a factory. At the factory, three things happen to the milk. It is pasteurized, homogenized, and fortified.

When milk is **pasteurized,** it is quickly heated and then cooled to kill germs. The germs killed by this process are harmful bacteria. If milk is not pasteurized, the germs in it can make people sick.

When milk is **homogenized,** it is pushed through tiny holes that break the fat in it down into tiny pieces. Homogenizing keeps milk from separating into skim milk and cream.

When milk is **fortified,** Vitamin D is added to it. **Vitamin D** is important. It helps the body to be healthy and to grow.

More ▶

Meets ISAT Standards
1.B.1a
1.B.1c
1.C.1a
1.C.1b
1.C.1d
2.B.1a

Reading Skills Review

Your Turn

Types of Milk

When you go to the grocery store, you will see different types of milk. This chart describes the differences:

Name	Amount of Milk Fat	Calories (per cup)
Whole milk	3.5 percent	150
Reduced-fat milk	2 percent	122
Low-fat milk	1 percent	102
Skim milk Fat-free milk	less than 0.5 percent	80

Stores also carry buttermilk. **Buttermilk** is made from nonfat or lowfat milk. Tiny creatures called **bacteria** are added to the milk. The bacteria are helpful "germs" in this case. They cause the milk to **curdle,** or become sour and lumpy. Buttermilk is great for cooking. There are also **sweetened, flavored milks,** such as chocolate milk and strawberry milk.

More ▶

Milk and Health

The U.S. government says that people should drink three glasses of milk or eat three servings of dairy products every day. Milk has lots of **calcium.** Calcium helps to build strong bones and teeth. Milk also has important vitamins.

Some people are allergic to milk. Others are lactose intolerant. This means that their bodies cannot break down the **lactose,** or milk sugar, in milk. These people have to get their calcium and vitamin D from other foods. Green vegetables, such as broccoli and spinach, are good sources of calcium. People who cannot drink milk should eat plenty of these vegetables.

Meets ISAT Standards
1.B.1a
1.B.1c
1.C.1a
1.C.1b
1.C.1d
2.B.1a

Active Reading

When you read something, you won't always have the time or space to take the kinds of notes you just made about the article on milk. You are more likely to remember what you read, however, if you stop and ask yourself about it every now and then. If you have trouble summing up what the writer said, try stopping more often.

It is a good idea to take some notes while you read. **Notes** are simply short reminders. You will learn more about notetaking in the next unit. For now, just remember that it is a good idea to read with a pencil and piece of paper beside you. When you read something important, make a note of it. Taking notes is especially important when you are reading for a test.

Here is an example of one student's notes on one paragraph from "Make Mine Milk":

One Student's Notes

Dairy cows
—Most in U.S. = Holsteins
—Holstein white w/black spots
—1 cow can make 2,300+ gal. milk/yr. (about 100 glasses/day!)
—Other dairy cows: Guernseys, Jerseys, Brown Swiss, Ayrshires

After Reading

After you read, you need to reflect and respond. When you **reflect** on something, you think about it. When you **respond** to something, you make a connection and take some action because of it. This chart shows some of the ways that you can reflect and respond:

Meets ISAT
Standards
1.B.1a
1.B.1c
1.C.1a
1.C.1b
1.C.1d
2.B.1a
3.C.1a
3.C.1b
4.B.1a
4.B.1b
5.C.1a

What to Do After Reading

Reflecting

1. **Try to summarize the reading.** In other words, think about what its main idea was. How would you answer the question if someone asked you, "What was that reading about?"

2. **Answer your prereading questions.** Think about the questions that you came up with when you first scanned the piece. Did the reading answer those questions? If so, how?

3. **Judge, or evaluate, the reading.** Think about what you liked or disliked about the reading. Think about what the writer seemed to do well, or not so well. This is called judging, or **evaluating,** the reading.

Responding

1. Talk about the reading with your classmates or friends or family.

2. Make a poster about the reading.

3. Do an oral report on the reading. Tell your classmates all about it.

4. Make a graphic organizer like those on pages 187–91 of this book.

5. Draw a picture related to the reading.

6. Write about the reading. A good place to write about it is in your journal. When you write about the reading, refer to specific parts of it. In your writing, you can summarize the reading. You can judge it. You can argue with the author. You can explain your own ideas about the topic.

Reading Skills Review 119

Your Turn

Exercise A One way to respond to a reading is to make a poster. Look back over the selection about milk in the previous exercise (pages 112–17). Then make a poster about ONE of these subjects:

- Common dairy products
- What happens to milk before you bring it home from the store
- Types of milk

Exercise B To respond to a reading, you can create a graphic organizer. One type of graphic organizer is the word web. To make a word web, you begin by writing a topic at the center of a piece of paper and circling it, like this:

(PIZZA)

Then, around the topic, you write related ideas, like this:

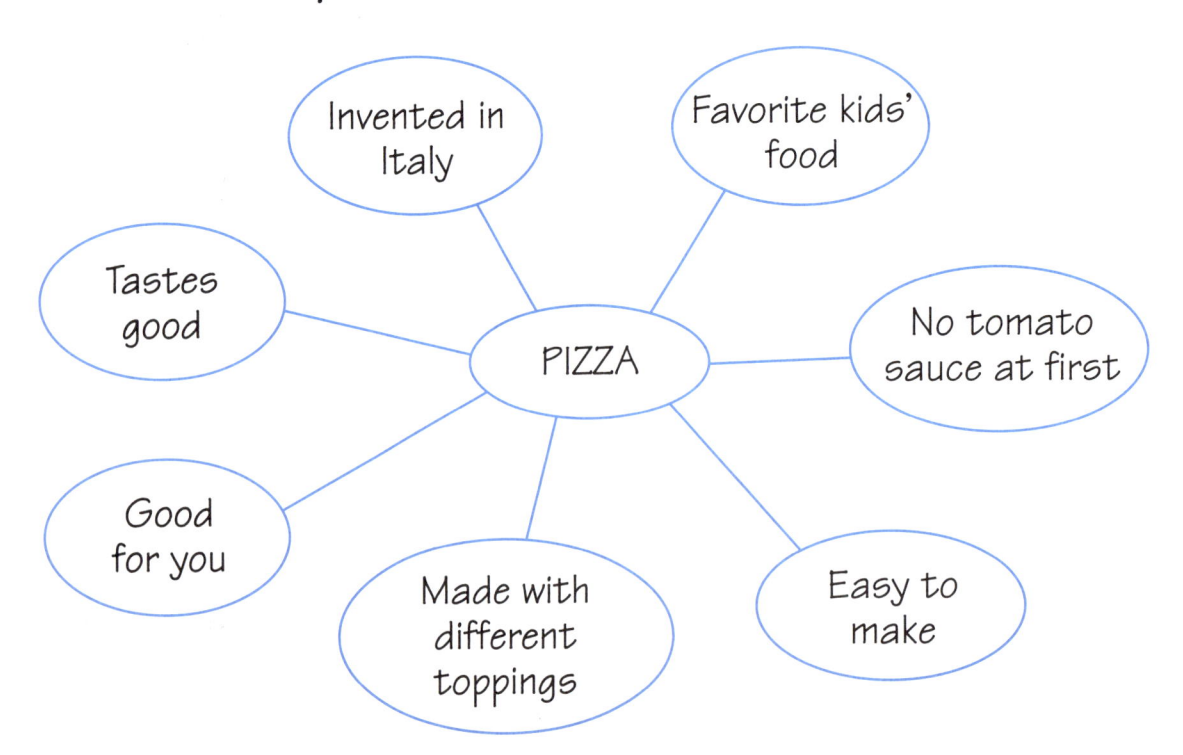

- Invented in Italy
- Favorite kids' food
- Tastes good
- No tomato sauce at first
- Good for you
- Made with different toppings
- Easy to make

PIZZA

120 AIM Higher! ISAT Language Arts Review

Reread this paragraph from the selection on milk. Then make a word web about Holstein cows.

Meets ISAT Standards
1.B.1a
1.B.1c
1.C.1f

In the United States, most dairy cows are Holsteins. A Holstein is white with black spots. The spots are different on every Holstein. So, a cow's spots are like fingerprints on a person! Holsteins make lots and lots of milk. A single cow can produce 2,305 gallons of milk a year. That's more than one hundred glasses of milk every day! To make that much milk, a cow must drink enough water every day to fill half a bathtub! Other types of dairy cow include Guernseys, Jerseys, Brown Swiss, and Ayrshires.

(HOLSTEIN COWS)

Chapter 5

I Think I've Got It!

Reading Comprehension

What is **reading comprehension?** Simply put, it is understanding what you read. In this chapter, you will learn about what to pay attention to as you read. What you learn in this chapter will improve your understanding of your reading. In other words, it will increase your comprehension.

Pay Attention to What's Important

Read this very short story:

> One day, Sam went to see his friend Ragnar. Ragnar was a very special guy. In fact, he was an alien. He came from a planet far, far away. Ragnar looked like everyone else on Earth. Most people had no idea he was an alien because he wore a fake face. Sometimes he said or did strange things, though.
>
> Sam rang Ragnar's bell. After a second or two, Ragnar answered the door. Ragnar had a book in his hand.
>
> "Oh. I see you've been reading," said Sam.
>
> "That's right," said Ragnar. "I love your Earth books."
>
> "Which one are you reading now?" Sam asked.
>
> "Oh. This is *The Magician's Nephew*, by C. S. Lewis."
>
> "I know that book," Sam said. "It's really great."
>
> "I, too, thought it interesting," said Ragnar.
>
> "What did you like most about it?" Sam asked.
>
> "Oh, that's easy," said Ragnar. "I liked the commas."

More ▶

"What do you mean, 'the commas'?" Sam asked.

"The commas," said Ragnar. "You know, those little squiggly things that look like this." Ragnar drew a big comma in the air with his left hand. "Did you know," said Ragnar, "that this book has exactly 153 commas in it? Isn't that great?"

"You must be kidding," Sam said. "Why is that great?"

"Well," said Ragnar, "suppose that you add up the numbers 1 and 5 and 3: 1 + 5 + 3. You get the number 9. And 153 can be divided evenly by 9."

"Wow, Ragnar. That's really interesting," Sam said, raising his eyebrows.

"That's not all," said Ragnar. He was so excited, his face almost fell off. "Suppose you turn around 153. You get 351. If you add 153 and 351, you get 504. Now, 504 times 504 is the same as 288 times 882, and, of course, 882 is 288 turned around. You see, 153 is a fascinating number of commas! And 153 + 315 + 531 = 351 + 135 + 513! Isn't that amazing?"

Sam stood quiet for a moment, thinking. Then he said, "Ragnar, I don't think you get it."

"What do you mean?" asked Ragnar.

"Well, what was the story in the book? Who were the characters? What was the main idea?" asked Sam.

"Oh, I didn't pay attention to any of that," said Ragnar.

"You didn't? Well, what did you pay attention to?"

"The commas, of course," said Ragnar. "And also the number of periods and the sizes of the letters. Very interesting."

Ragnar had a couple of things to learn about reading. But he was really good at math. And he probably knew more about the commas in that book than anyone.

Reading Skills Review 123

Reading Comprehension

In the story you just read, Ragnar read a book very closely. However, he did not read it in the right way. He did not pay attention to what was important. Here are some things that you should pay attention to when reading:

What to Pay Attention to When Reading

Main Idea	The main point that the writer makes
Sequence	The order of the events
Causes	What makes things in the reading happen
Effects	What happens as a result of other events
Vocabulary	The meanings of new words
Theme	The lesson or moral of a story; the writer's message

During your years in school, you will sometimes take reading tests. These tests often will ask you questions about the items in the chart above.

124 AIM Higher! ISAT Language Arts Review

Look for Main Ideas

Often, reading tests ask about the main idea. The **main idea** is what the piece is mostly about.

Read the short piece below. Then think about the question that follows it.

Meets ISAT
Standards
1.A.1a
1.A.1b
1.B.1c
1.C.1b
1.C.1d
2.A.1a

> Many of the old Greek and Roman stories deal with people who are changed in some way. For example, in one story, a girl brags about her weaving. She is changed into a spider. In another, a girl gossips too much. She becomes an echo. She is doomed to repeat what other people have said forever. In yet another story, a boy thinks that he is beautiful. He likes looking at his face in the water. A god turns him into a flower that grows by ponds and streams.

Think about this question:

What is the main idea of this paragraph?
- Ⓐ A girl is turned into a spider because of her bragging.
- Ⓑ Many old Greek and Roman stories are about people who are turned into something else.
- Ⓒ A boy who loves how he looks is turned into a flower.
- Ⓓ A voice that repeats what others say is called an echo.

ANSWER: Choices A, C, and D are all true. However, each of these answers tells about only part of the reading. The main idea is what the piece as a whole is mostly about. Choose the answer that best describes the whole reading. Choice B describes the whole piece. Therefore, B is the correct answer.

Reading Skills Review 125

Reading Comprehension

Questions that ask about the main idea can be written in several ways. Here are some possibilities:

Questions about the Main Idea

- What is the piece mostly about?
- What would be a good title for this piece?
- Which sentence best sums up the piece?
- What is the main idea?

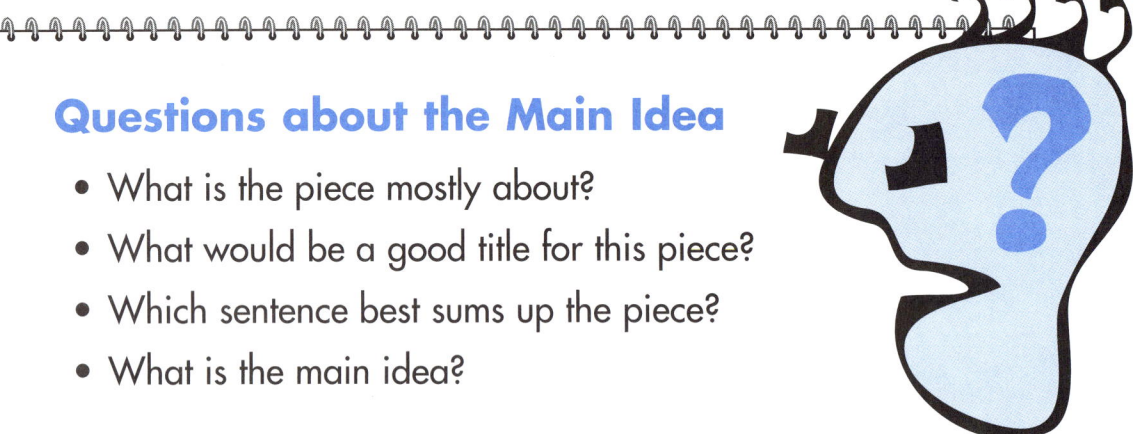

Even though these questions are written differently, they all ask about the piece as a whole. Here are some strategies for answering questions about the main idea:

Answering Questions about the Main Idea

- Look for words in the question that tell you that it is about the main idea. Such words include *main idea, subject, topic, mostly about, theme, lesson,* and *as a whole.*
- Scan the whole selection. Look quickly at all its parts. These include the title, introduction, headings, highlighted words, captions, and conclusion. These parts can give you clues as to what the whole selection is about. If a question asks about the main idea of a certain paragraph, read that paragraph carefully.
- Rule out answers that you know are wrong. Then choose the best answer from the ones that are left.
- Remember that an answer can be true but still may not tell the main idea.

126 AIM Higher! ISAT Language Arts Review

Your Turn

Exercise Read each short selection and answer the question that follows it. Fill in the circle next to the correct answer to each question.

Meets ISAT
Standards
1.B.1c
1.C.1b
1.C.1d

Little green sea turtles take an amazing journey after they are born. The mother turtle lays her eggs in a hole that she digs on the beach. When a baby turtle breaks out of its egg, it walks down to the ocean. Then it swims away. It floats and swims along, eating tiny sea creatures and plants. A few years later, after a journey of as much as 2,000 miles, a female turtle returns to the place where she was hatched to lay her own eggs.

1. What is this passage MOSTLY about?
   Ⓐ Turtles are born from eggs.
   Ⓑ Baby turtles eat tiny sea creatures and plants.
   Ⓒ Turtles lay their eggs on beaches.
   Ⓓ Green sea turtles make amazing journeys.

When you think of an elephant, you probably think right away of its trunk and its large ears. An elephant uses its big, flat ears to cool itself off. When an elephant gets hot, it flaps its ears like fans. This makes a breeze that cools the elephant. Also, when an elephant flaps its ears, a lot of air passes over the ears. This makes the elephant feel cooler. The African elephant has very large ears shaped like triangles. The Indian elephant has smaller, rounder ears.

2. What is the main subject of this paragraph?
   Ⓐ the differences between African and Indian elephants
   Ⓑ how an elephant's ears help it stay cool
   Ⓒ the homeland of the African elephant
   Ⓓ the uses of elephants for work and sport

More ▶

Reading Skills Review 127

Your Turn

The Internet is the most powerful method of communication ever invented. Like magazines and newspapers, the Internet shows pictures and text. Unlike the pictures and text in magazines and newspapers, those on the Internet can be sent around the world in seconds. Like telephones, the Internet allows people to send messages to one another over distance. Unlike telephone conversations, Internet chat is very cheap.

3. What would be a good title for this selection?
- Ⓐ "Internet Telephones"
- Ⓑ "Why the Internet Is Better Than Magazines"
- Ⓒ "The Most Powerful Method of Communication"
- Ⓓ "The Costs per Minute of Internet Chat"

Reading Comprehension

Look for Significant Details

Sometimes a test question will ask about an important piece of information from a selection. Such a piece of information is called a **significant detail.**

Read the short piece below. Then think about the question that follows it.

> Beauregarde, our beagle, has a terrible fear of cooking. Whenever Dad starts to make breakfast or dinner, Beauregarde runs to the door and begs to be let out. Why? Well, Dad is a great cook, but he is also a bit sloppy. When he spills something in the oven, the oven starts to smoke. Twice, when he was cooking, smoke filled the house, and our fire alarms went off. The fire alarms make a really loud noise. The noise must have hurt Beauregarde's ears. Now, our dog runs for the door any time he sees Dad with a ladle in his hand.

Meets ISAT Standards
1.B.1c
1.C.1b
1.C.1d

Think about this question:

How many times did the fire alarms go off?
- Ⓐ once
- Ⓑ twice
- Ⓒ three times
- Ⓓ four times

Reading Skills Review 129

Reading Comprehension

ANSWER: To find the answer, look for a key word or words in the question. **Key words** are important words from a selection or question. A pair of key words from the question is *fire alarms*. Scan the passage, looking for this pair of key words. When you find it, read carefully. In this way, you can find the sentence "Twice, when he was cooking, smoke filled the house, and our fire alarms went off." Therefore, B is the correct answer.

Here are some strategies for answering questions about significant details:

Answering Questions about Significant Details

- Look for one or more key words in the question.
- Scan the selection until you find those key words in the text.
- To find your answer, read carefully the sentence or sentences that contain the key word or words.

130 AIM Higher! ISAT Language Arts Review

Your Turn

Exercise Read each short selection and answer the question that follows it. Fill in the circle next to the correct answer to each question.

Meets ISAT Standards
1.B.1c
1.C.1b
1.C.1d

    The Chrysler Building, which is 1,046 feet tall, was built in New York City in 1930. At that time, there was no taller structure in the world. The Chrysler Building was the tallest building in the world for less than a year, though. In 1931, the Empire State Building was completed. That skyscraper, 1,250 feet tall, was the tallest building in the world until 1972, when the first tower of the World Trade Center was finished. Today, there are even taller buildings. For example, the two Petronas Towers, in Malaysia, are each 1,483 feet tall.

1. In what year was the Empire State Building built?
   - Ⓐ 1483
   - Ⓑ 1930
   - Ⓒ 1972
   - Ⓓ 1931

More ▶

Reading Skills Review 131

Your Turn

Some ants spend a lot of their time building, repairing, and changing their nests. These nests are networks of underground tunnels that connect rooms called chambers. Some chambers are for eggs. Some chambers are for storing food. There are special chambers just for baby ants. In some ant nests, there are special chambers where the ants hibernate, or sleep during the winter. Throughout the rest of the year, the ants work on the nest. They build new tunnels and repair walls. They dig out new chambers and fill in old ones. All this building and repairing of tunnels and chambers keeps ants really busy.

2. What do some ants do during the winter?
- Ⓐ build tiny igloos
- Ⓑ rubs sticks together to make fire
- Ⓒ move to Florida
- Ⓓ hibernate

Reading Comprehension

Look for Sequences

Some readings describe events, or happenings. These usually occur in a particular order, or **sequence**. Here, for example, is a series of events that is out of order:

—enjoy the ice cream cone
—wave down the ice cream truck
—hear the bell of the ice cream truck
—buy an ice cream cone
—wait for the truck to stop

Here is the same group of events, put in correct order, or sequence:

—hear the bell of the ice cream truck
—wave down the ice cream truck
—wait for the truck to stop
—buy an ice cream cone
—enjoy the ice cream cone

Read the short piece below. Then think about the question that follows it.

Meets ISAT Standards
1.B.1c
1.C.1b
1.C.1d

The owner of a candy store in Scarborough, Maine, decided to create a special attraction. First, she hired a sculptor from an art school. The sculptor traveled to Freeport, Maine, to study a stuffed moose there. Then he came back to the candy store and started work. He built a wire frame. Then he covered the frame with chocolate. The result was a 1,700-pound, life-sized chocolate moose named Lenny. This moose is now on display at the store in Scarborough, Maine.

Reading Skills Review

Reading Comprehension

Think about this question:

Which event happened FIRST?
- Ⓐ The sculptor traveled to Freeport, Maine.
- Ⓑ The sculptor made a wire frame of a moose.
- Ⓒ The finished moose was displayed at the candy store.
- Ⓓ The candy store owner hired a sculptor from an art school.

ANSWER: All of the events listed as answers actually happened. All are mentioned in the paragraph. However, the first of the events is D, so D is the correct answer.

Here are some strategies for answering questions about sequence:

Answering Questions about Sequence

- Look for key words in the question that tell you that it is about sequence. Such words include *first, last,* and *when*.
- Pay attention to the order in which things happen when you read.
- Look for words like *first, next, then, finally, as a result,* and *now* that tell you when things happen.
- Remember that sometimes writers do not necessarily tell about events in order. For example, a writer might start with the last event and then tell about the events leading up to it.
- If the question gives one event and asks you to find another before or after it, find one or more key words in the question or answer choices. Scan the reading to find the key word or words. Then read carefully to find your answer.

Your Turn

Exercise Read each short selection and answer the question that follows it. Fill in the circle next to the correct answer to each question.

Meets ISAT Standards
1.B.1c
1.C.1b
1.C.1d

It took over twenty years to build the Great Pyramids of Egypt. Historians believe that about 100,000 men worked to build the pyramids. Scientists have some idea about how the pyramids were built. First, the workers cleared a flat area for the pyramid. On this flat surface, they placed the first layer of stones. Then they built a ramp around the edge. Next, they moved the second layers of stones up the ramp and put them in place. As each layer was put into place, the workers added another ramp. Eventually, the ramps wound around the pyramid in a giant spiral. Finally, the workers placed a gold-covered stone at the top.

1. According to the paragraph, what was the LAST step in the construction of a pyramid?
   Ⓐ Workers built ramps around the pyramid.
   Ⓑ Workers held a ceremony to dedicate the pyramid.
   Ⓒ Workers placed a gold-covered stone at the top.
   Ⓓ Workers placed a layer of stones on a flat surface.

More ▶

Reading Skills Review 135

Your Turn

Today in art class, we made placemats. First, the art teacher handed out large sheets of paper to everyone. Then she put pens, pencils, markers, and crayons on our tables. Next, she told us to think of our favorite food. After we decided on our favorite food, we had to draw a picture of it on the paper. I spent a long time drawing a picture of a hamburger. I even included some lettuce and a slice of tomato! Then I used markers to color in my drawing. Finally, the art teacher used a machine to put clear plastic covers on our placemats. I think I'll give mine to my dad.

2. What did the art teacher do right after she put pens, pencils, markers, and crayons on the tables?

   Ⓐ She handed out large sheets of paper.
   Ⓑ She told the students to draw pictures of hamburgers.
   Ⓒ She covered the students' drawings with clear plastic.
   Ⓓ She told the students to think of their favorite food.

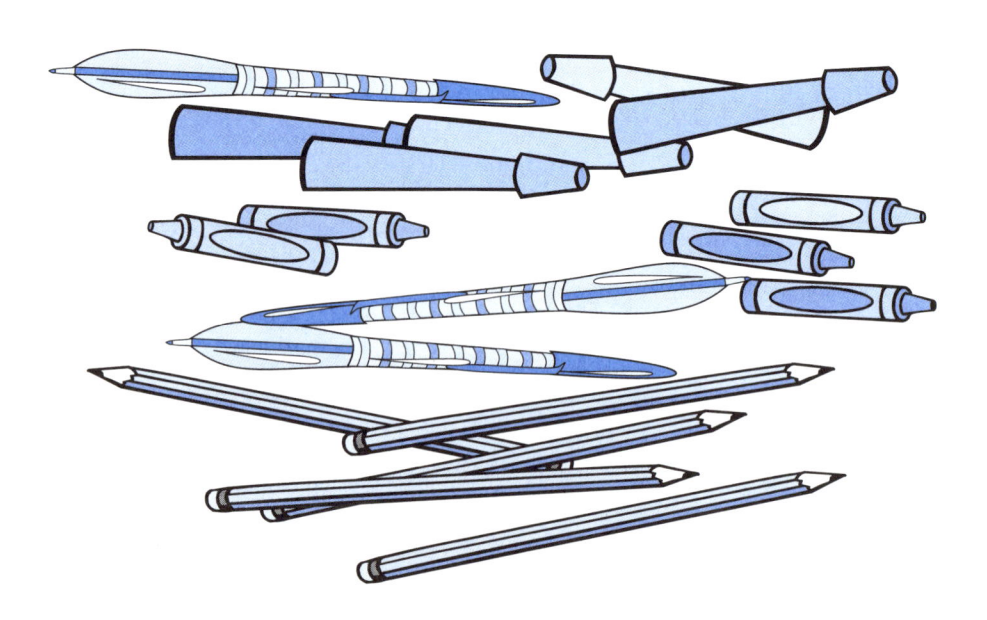

Reading Comprehension

Look for Causes and Effects

Cause and effect is a relationship between events. Good readers pay close attention to cause-and-effect relationships. A **cause** is the reason why something happens. Sometimes, an event has more than one cause. An **effect** is something that happens because of something else. An event may also have more than one effect.

Here are some examples of causes and effects:

Cause	Effect
No rain for a long time	→ Plants dry up and die
Loud noise	→ Headache
Studying hard, getting lots of rest, and eating well	→ Doing your best on a test

Meets ISAT Standards
1.B.1c
1.C.1b
1.C.1d

Read the short piece below. Then think about the question that follows it.

The world, as a whole, is getting warmer each year. This increase in temperature is called global warming. What causes global warming? One cause is the burning of fuel. When people burn fuel, such as wood, oil, and gas, they produce more than heat and smoke. Burning these things also produces invisible leftovers. Some of the leftovers in the air are called greenhouse gases. These gases enter the atmosphere. They trap the sun's heat and keep it close to the Earth. This makes the Earth warmer.

Reading Skills Review

Reading Comprehension

Think about this question:

Which of the following is a cause of global warming?
- Ⓐ the Ice Age
- Ⓑ greenhouse gases
- Ⓒ scientists
- Ⓓ the Earth's becoming hotter

ANSWER: Answer A is obviously incorrect. In an Ice Age, large parts of the Earth are covered with ice. The Earth is colder, not warmer. Answer C is also obviously incorrect. Scientists are not mentioned in the paragraph as causing the warming. Answer D is incorrect because the Earth's becoming hotter is an effect—not a cause—of global warming. Answer B, "greenhouse gases," is correct.

Here are some strategies for answering questions about cause-and-effect relationships.

Meets ISAT Standards
1.B.1c
1.C.1b
1.C.1d

Answering Questions about Causes and Effects

- As you read, look for key words used in descriptions of causes and effects. Such words include *why, because, reason, therefore, as a result, cause, effect, consequently,* and *so.*

- Read the question carefully to see if it is asking about a cause or an effect. Questions about causes often contains words like *why, what reason,* or *what caused.* Questions about effects often begin with words like *what happened as a result of, what was the result of, what happened because,* or *what is an effect of.*

- Remember that events can happen one after the other without being related by cause and effect. Ask yourself, "Did one event make the other happen?"

- Remember that an event can have several causes, and one event can also have several effects.

Effect

Cause

Reading Skills Review

Your Turn

Exercise Read each short selection and answer the question that follows it. Fill in the circle next to the correct answer to each question.

During a typical day, the heart of a healthy human beats about 100,000 times. With each beat, the heart pumps blood through the body. There are red blood cells and white blood cells in the blood. The main job of red blood cells is to carry oxygen to different parts of the body. The heart pumps blood through the lungs. In the lungs, the red blood cells absorb oxygen. Then the blood travels back to the heart. The heart pushes the blood, with its red blood cells full of oxygen, into the body. As the blood travels through the body, the red blood cells deliver oxygen to other kinds of cells. Without oxygen, these cells would die. After the red blood cells deliver all of the oxygen they are carrying, the blood returns to the heart. Then the heart pumps the blood into the lungs to begin all over again.

1. What happens if the cells of the body do not receive oxygen?
   - Ⓐ They turn blue.
   - Ⓑ They die.
   - Ⓒ They travel to the lungs.
   - Ⓓ They turn into red blood cells.

Deep underwater, where no sunlight can reach, there are some very special creatures. These creatures make their own light. Some deepsea fish, called anglerfish, dangle their own lures to attract other fish. The Atlantic footballfish, for example, has a lure hanging from its head that glows at the tip. Any smaller fish that comes over to the lure will probably be eaten. Other fish, called flashlight fish, light up so brightly that they can be seen from about one hundred feet away. Scientists believe that one effect of their lighting up is that it confuses animals that want to eat them. This helps to keep flashlight fish safe. There are also tiny plants in the ocean that glow in the dark. Some of these tiny plants live in jellyfish. The glow attracts food for the jellyfish.

2. What happens when a flashlight fish lights up?
   Ⓐ Animals that want to eat it may become confused.
   Ⓑ It attracts tiny plants that it can eat.
   Ⓒ Jellyfish keep away from it.
   Ⓓ It can be seen from over 200 feet away.

Reading Comprehension

Look for Context Clues

The **vocabulary** of a reading selection is the words that are used in it. Sometimes, as you read you will come across words that you do not know. You can figure out what unfamiliar vocabulary words mean by looking at **context clues.** These are words and phrases (groups of words) around the unfamiliar word that give hints about its meaning.

Read the short piece below. Then think about the question that follows it.

> Would you like to work in the world of fashion? There are many possible jobs in this field. Some people design fabrics that are made into high-fashion clothes. Some people design the clothes themselves. Some designers specialize in particular kinds of clothes, such as hats, coats, or evening dresses. Other people work as tailors, actually creating the clothing from other people's designs. Still others work as models. Some writers work as reporters for the fashion press. Some people work in marketing. They sell lines or brands of clothing to stores. Buyers choose the clothes to be sold in a store each season. Still other people work in sales, helping customers on the floor of stores where high-quality clothes are sold.

When there are no hints to a word's meaning in its context (the words nearby), sometimes you can figure out what it means from its **word parts.** For example, *impossible* = *im* + *possible*. Since *im–* means "not," you know that *impossible* means "not possible." See Chapter 3, "Sound Off! Sounds, Spelling, and Word Parts," for more information on using word parts.

Think about this question:

> Meets ISAT Standards
> 1.A.1a
> 1.A.1b
> 1.B.1c

5. In the high-fashion world, what does a *tailor* do?
   - Ⓐ design, create, and sell high-fashion clothes
   - Ⓑ model high-fashion clothes
   - Ⓒ make clothing from other people's designs
   - Ⓓ write books of advice for women in business

ANSWER: Answer A is incorrect because it describes many of the jobs in the world of fashion. Answer B is also wrong. Models do the modeling, not tailors. Answer D is obviously incorrect because the paragraph says nothing about writing books of advice for women in business. If you scan the paragraph for the key word *tailor*, you will find this sentence: "Other people work as tailors, actually creating the clothing from other people's designs." So, answer C is correct.

Reading Skills Review 143

Reading Comprehension

Types of Context Clue

There are many types of context clue. Sometimes, an unfamiliar word is defined directly.

A *crank* is someone with crazy ideas.

Sometimes a word is defined by examples.

A *crank* is someone who believes that people are being stolen away by aliens or that magnets can cure cancer or other ideas like that.

Sometimes a word is defined by comparing it to something that is similar.

Jane was *miffed*. Her little brother was also angry.

A word can also be defined by contrasting it with something that means the opposite.

Jane was *disconsolate*. Her little brother, on the other hand, was quite happy.

Here are some strategies for answering questions about vocabulary:

Answering Questions about Vocabulary Defined in Context

- Scan the selection until you find the unfamiliar word.
- Study the words around the unfamiliar word. Look for clues to the word's meaning.
- Look for these types of context clue: direct definition, examples, comparisons, and contrasts.

Your Turn

Exercise Read each short selection below and answer the question that follows it. Fill in the circle next to the correct answer to each question.

Meets ISAT Standards
1.A.1b
1.B.1c

The wizard ordered Dorothy and her friends to bring back the broom of the Wicked Witch of the West. They tried to talk the wizard out of it, but *he was resolute.*

1. What is the meaning of *he was resolute?*
   - Ⓐ He was very nice.
   - Ⓑ His mind could not be changed.
   - Ⓒ He was very powerful.
   - Ⓓ He was green and surrounded by smoke.

In most comic book series, a superhero battles at least one *villain.* In *Superman,* the main villain is Lex Luthor. In *Batman,* there are quite a few, such as the Joker and the Riddler.

2. What does *villain* mean?
   - Ⓐ leader
   - Ⓑ friend
   - Ⓒ banker
   - Ⓓ bad guy

There's nothing quite as satisfactory as a *warbler,* or songbird, for lifting your spirits.

3. What does *warbler* mean?
   - Ⓐ whistler
   - Ⓑ waterfowl
   - Ⓒ healer
   - Ⓓ songbird

Mr. Morales's grandfather was a great *orator.* His father also gave wonderful speeches at large gatherings.

4. What does *orator* mean?
   - Ⓐ teacher
   - Ⓑ general
   - Ⓒ cook
   - Ⓓ public speaker

Reading Skills Review

Reading Comprehension

Look for the Theme

You already know about main ideas. A main idea is an important point that a writer wants to make. A main idea in a story is called a **theme.** In writing about real events, a writer often states the main idea directly. In stories, a writer may let the reader figure out the main idea on his or her own. The main idea, or theme, in a story is often a lesson that the story teaches. Sometimes this is a lesson learned by the main character.

You may remember the story of Chicken Little. This is a well-known children's story. In one version of the story, an acorn falls on Chicken Little's head. The chicken runs off and starts telling everyone she meets that the sky is falling. All the animals she meets believe her. They become really scared and follow along to tell the other animals. Eventually, the animals come upon the fox. The fox tells the animals that he knows a place where they can be safe. He leads the animals into his den, where he eats them for dinner.

What is the theme of this story? Well, one theme might be that "You shouldn't believe everything you hear." Another might be, "Don't panic and jump to the wrong conclusion." Yet another might be, "What you fear most might not be the real danger."

Think about this question:

Which of the following is a possible theme of the story "Chicken Little"?

- Ⓐ If the sky is falling on your head, you had better hide.
- Ⓑ Act first and ask questions later.
- Ⓒ If you believe everything you hear, you are likely to get into trouble.
- Ⓓ Even dumb creatures can have something important to teach you.

Meets ISAT Standards
1.B.1c
1.C.1b
2.A.1a

ANSWER: Answer A is not correct because, in the story, finding a place to hide leads to disaster. Answer B is not correct because all the animals except the fox do this and end up in trouble. Answer D is not correct because the animals in the story make the mistake of listening to Chicken Little, who is not very bright. That leaves Answer C. This answer is correct because the animals who believe what they are told without question are the ones that are eaten.

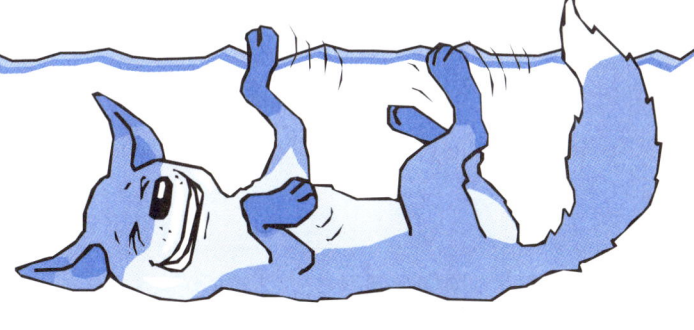

Reading Skills Review

Reading Comprehension

Here are some strategies for answering questions about theme:

Answering Questions about Theme

- Ask yourself, "What does the main character learn in this story?"

- Ask yourself, "What message is this story trying to teach me and other readers?"

- If you do not know the answer right away, get rid of obviously wrong answers first. These are answers that do not fit the facts in the story.

- Remember that questions about theme might be presented as questions about the main idea. They also might be about the lesson or moral that a character or the reader learns.

Your Turn

Exercise Read this story. Then answer the questions that follow it. Fill in the circle next to the correct answer to each question.

Meets ISAT
Standards
1.B.1c
1.C.1b
2.A.1a

Where Have All the Fairies Gone?
by Robin Lamb

I was four years old when Dad first told me about the fairies. We had just moved from the city to New Hampshire. Dad said it was quieter and more peaceful in the country. But I didn't like it. Moving meant that I had to leave my Tia Rosita. It also meant that Dad left early in the morning and came home late at night. He had to drive a long way and then catch a train to go to work. I saw him less, and that made me mad.

One Saturday, not long after we moved, we were driving to a hardware store together. The nearest store was pretty far away. Where we lived, there were lots of woods and stone walls and roads with no one on them. I sat on the passenger side watching the trees whiz by.

"Why did we have to move from the city, Daddy?" I asked.

"Well, honey . . . Why do you ask? Did you like it better in Boston?"

"You bet!" I said.

"Boston is nice. That's true," said Dad. "But your Mom and I think it will be good for you to grow up in the country."

"Why?"

"Well, the air is cleaner. And there is less traffic and noise. And it's safer."

"Safer?" I asked.

More ▶

Your Turn

"Well, that is what we think. And besides, here you have a better chance of meeting the fairies." Dad winked at me as he said this.

"Fairies? What are fairies?" I asked.

"Well, fairies are little people—about half as tall as you when they're full grown."

"You're joking, Daddy."

"No. Not at all," he assured me. "You see, long, long ago, back when the world was young, people and fairies used to mingle."

"What does *mingle* mean?" I asked.

"That means that they used to see each other and talk and socialize," he explained. "They even did things together like have councils—big meetings. But then people started getting uppity. They started driving cars and building cities and factories. Then the fairies went into hiding. You see, fairies hate all that," he explained.

"Hate what?" I asked.

"Technology," Dad answered. "If there is anything that fairies hate, it is computers and cars and buses and airplanes and televisions and cell phones and parking meters and electric lights and . . . ."

"Trucks?"

"Yes, and trucks."

"And game systems?" I asked.

"Oh yes," he replied. "Fairies hate game systems. Almost as much as they hate cell phones and PDAs."

"What's a PDA?" I asked.

More ▶

"You know, that little computer notepad that Daddy writes on all the time."

"Oh, yeah. Why do fairies hate technology?"

"Well. I don't know. I guess fairies just think that the moon and the stars are better than electric lights. And a fairy would probably tell you that dancing in a circle is better than any old game you can play on a game system."

"So, are there any fairies around these days?" I asked.

"Oh, sure. Lots and lots of fairies. They just… Well, they are very good at hiding. You know how I know that they are really good at hiding?"

"How?" I asked.

"Well, you've never seen a fairy, have you?" Dad asked.

"No."

"Well, then, they must be pretty good at it!" said Dad.

"But Daddy," I said, "If no one has ever seen a fairy, how do you know that there are fairies at all?"

"Well, I thought I saw one once," Dad answered. "Caught just a glimpse of a coat tail rounding a big old woodpile on my grandfather's farm. But that was years ago. Sometimes, you know, people walking in the woods find on the ground circles of extra green grass called fairy rings. They say that's where the fairies have been dancing. And where the fairies have danced, mushrooms grow on top of the ring."

"Is that because fairies are magic?" I asked.

More ▶

Reading Skills Review   151

Your Turn

"Very, very magical," said Dad. "And sometimes at night people see little lights in the woods—fairy lights, they call them. People, though, are big and clumsy, and they make a lot of noise. By the time they get close enough to see the fairies, the fairies have put their lights out and scampered away."

"I would love to see a fairy," I said.

"Well, that's why we moved to the country. At least it's one reason. We thought we'd have a much better chance of seeing fairies out here than in the city. Now keep your eyes peeled. You never know."

That was twenty-six years ago. Growing up in the country, I learned to make my own entertainment and to use my imagination. Needless to say, I can see fairies any time I please.

1. Which of the following is a theme of the story "Where Have All the Fairies Gone"?

    Ⓐ Technology has brought many good things to people.

    Ⓑ Fairies, elves, gnomes, trolls, and other imaginary creatures are just silly.

    Ⓒ Technology has had some bad consequences as well as good ones.

    Ⓓ People are too smart to believe in fairies anymore.

2. What lesson does Robin learn from his or her father?

    Ⓐ that there are no fairies

    Ⓑ that technology is a great blessing

    Ⓒ that life in the city is better than life in the country

    Ⓓ that the imagination is powerful

Chapter 6

The Truth and Then Some

Reading Nonfiction and Fiction

In the last two chapters, you have learned some important reading skills. You have learned how to preview a reading selection. You have learned how to read it actively. You have also learned how to respond to a selection after reading it. You have learned how to notice and think about main ideas, details, sequences, causes and effects, vocabulary, and themes. In this chapter, you are going to learn about some of the different kinds of reading selections that you will come across in school and on tests.

Meets ISAT
Standards
1.B.1b
1.B.1c
1.C.1b
2.A.1b

Reading Nonfiction and Fiction

Types of Writing

Two main types of writing are nonfiction and fiction.

Nonfiction is writing about real people, places, and events.

The purpose of some nonfiction writing is to tell a story. This type of nonfiction is called **narrative nonfiction.** Pay attention to the people, dates, times, and places, as well as to what happens and why.

EXAMPLES:

- an **autobiography,** or story of a real person's life as told by that person
- a **biography,** or story of a real person's life as told by someone else
- a **history,** or story about real events that took place in the past

In another type of nonfiction, the purpose is to inform or explain. This type of nonfiction is called **informative,** or **expository, nonfiction.**

EXAMPLES:

- a magazine article about a real-life subject like skateboarding
- a news story

The purpose of another type of nonfiction is to persuade readers to believe or do something. This is called **persuasive nonfiction.**

EXAMPLES:

- an editorial in a newspaper
- a campaign speech

Fiction is writing about imaginary people, places, and events.

EXAMPLES:

- a short story
- a novel

One great thing about reading is that no matter what you are interested in, you can find something to read that will interest you. There are many different kinds of writing for you to read. Besides nonfiction and fiction, there are other types of writing, as well. **Poetry** is writing in lines of verse instead of paragraphs. It uses the sounds of words, including rhythm, to create an effect. Examples of poetry range from a nursery rhyme to the lyrics to a popular song. A poem can tell a story or express the speaker's feelings about a person or subject. **Drama** is another type of writing. It is meant to be performed by actors on stage. Examples of drama include stage plays and screenplays for movies and television.

Meets ISAT Standards
1.B.1a
1.B.1b
1.B.1c
1.C.1a
1.C.1b
1.C.1f
2.A.1a
2.A.1b
2.A.1c

Reading Nonfiction Actively

As you have already learned, **nonfiction** is writing about real people, places, ideas, and events. Here are a few things that you should do when reading nonfiction:

Before Reading

Skim the piece. (Look it over quickly.) Ask yourself, what is this piece about? In other words, what is the **topic** of the piece of writing?

Think about what you already know about the topic.

Think of some questions that might be answered by the piece as you read it.

As you begin to read, **look for the thesis statement.** This is one or two sentences that tell the **main idea,** or most important idea, of the piece. The thesis statement is usually near the beginning.

More ▶

Reading Skills Review 155

Reading Nonfiction and Fiction

During Reading

As you read, think about what you are reading.
Use the active reading strategies:

- ✔ **Ask Questions**
- ✔ **Visualize**
- ✔ **Predict**
- ✔ **Summarize**
- ✔ **Make Connections**

Look for facts and opinions. Facts are statements that can be proved to be true. **Opinions** are statements that cannot be proved to be true or false. Informative nonfiction should have facts only. Persuasive nonfiction will have opinions that should be backed up with facts. Ask yourself whether the facts the writer mentions are accurate. Also ask whether the writer's opinions are backed up with facts.

After Reading

Think about the piece. Ask yourself these questions:

- ✔ What was the **thesis,** or main idea, of the piece?
- ✔ Did the writer support his or her thesis? How?
- ✔ What was the **purpose** of the piece? That is, what was the writer's reason for creating it? The purpose can be
    - to tell a story.
    - to inform (or provide information).
    - to persuade (to convince people to change their minds or to act in some way).
    - a combination of these purposes.

Judge the piece. Did the writer do a good job? Did you enjoy the piece? Think about the purpose. Was the writer able to do what he or she set out to do? Why, or why not?

Respond to the piece. Discuss it and/or write about it.

Your Turn

Exercise Read the piece of nonfiction that begins on the next page. Before, during, and after reading, follow the steps numbered in blue.

Before Reading

1. Look over the piece quickly. What is its topic?

   _____

   _____

2. Write two questions that you think will be answered when you read the piece.

   A. _____

   _____

   _____

   B. _____

   _____

   _____

Meets ISAT
Standards
1.B.1a
1.B.1c
1.C.1a
1.C.1b
1.C.1e
2.B.1a

More ▶

Reading Skills Review   157

Your Turn

During Reading

3. Read the first paragraph. After reading it, underline the thesis statement. This tells the main idea of the piece.

4. As you read the rest of the piece, write down your responses. Be an active reader: Question, visualize, summarize, predict, and make connections. Write at least five responses on the lines provided. One sample response has been provided to get you started.

Mars: When Do We Move In?
by Marion Bubriski

    There's no running water. The average temperature is minus 81 degrees. And, by the way, you can't breathe there. That's because there's almost no oxygen in the atmosphere. Sounds like a great place to live, right? Even though all these facts are true of Mars, scientists still think that people might live there one day.

    Human beings can't stay put. We've explored just about every inch of our planet. Almost every place on Earth where people can live, they do. People live in deserts, in the frozen north, and on islands in the middle of the Pacific Ocean. It is only natural that we should now look to other planets in space.

    Space really is the next frontier. Earth is big, but it is not big enough to hold everyone forever. Over time, the number of people on Earth gets larger and larger. One day, there will not be enough room

Your Notes and Comments

_____
_____
_____

Making Connections: _People living on Mars? That sounds like something out of a movie._

_____
_____
_____
_____
_____
_____

for all of us. That's why it is important to find other places where people can move.

If we look around our immediate neighborhood in space, we do not see much that looks promising. The moon is a just a cold hunk of rock. Venus, the second planet from the sun, is so hot that rocks on its surface melt. Mars, on the other hand, looks as if it might have some possibilities. For life to exist as it does on Earth, there must be water, oxygen, carbon, and nitrogen. All of these can be found on Mars. However, they are frozen in ice caps at the poles or inside rocks. Mars today is not only very cold. It also changes from very high to very low temperatures. No living thing that we know about could live on Mars today.

The question, then, is how could we make Mars livable? One way to make it possible for people to live on Mars someday would be to build biospheres. Another way would be to terraform the planet.

Let's look at each of these ideas:

A **biosphere** is a living environment. To create one on Mars, it would have to be completely sealed off from the outside. Inside the biosphere would be all the things that people need for living, including running water

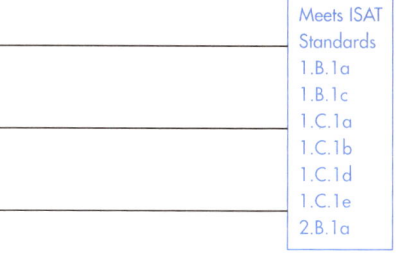

Meets ISAT
Standards
1.B.1a
1.B.1c
1.C.1a
1.C.1b
1.C.1d
1.C.1e
2.B.1a

More ▶

Reading Skills Review 159

Your Turn

and an atmosphere that has oxygen. People living in the biosphere could grow plants. The plants would make oxygen and could serve as food for the people.

Building a biosphere on Mars, however, is not so simple. First, it would be very complicated and expensive to build a biosphere just to house a few people. Second, over time, even in a carefully planned biosphere, waste products and dangerous pollutants would build up in a closed-off environment. Third, shipping supplies to people living in a biosphere on Mars would take a lot of money and effort.

Another way to make Mars livable would be to terraform it. What does the word *terraform* mean? *Terra* is a Latin word meaning "Earth." To *terraform* is to form, or make, something Earthlike. Scientists have been thinking for some time about how they could make the planet Mars more like Earth. To do that, they would have to heat up the planet and create a thick atmosphere around it. Then they would have to introduce living things to Mars.

Two suggestions have been made for terraforming Mars. One is to put giant mirrors in orbit around the planet. These mirrors would reflect light from the sun onto the poles of the planet Mars. This would melt the Martian ice caps. Melting ice would release running water and the gases needed to create an atmosphere. Another suggestion is to send rockets to push asteroids around in space, so that they would slam into the planet Mars. If asteroids slammed into the planet, the explosions would create heat. This heat would release gases from the Martian rocks. Creating a thicker atmosphere would be like wrapping Mars in a blanket. The atmosphere would keep more of the sun's heat near the planet. This increased heat would melt more of the ice caps. The melting of the ice caps would create more atmosphere and more heat. By this method, over time, Mars would become warmer. When the planet's atmosphere got warm enough and thick enough, people could send bacteria there that would make oxygen. Eventually, the planet would be made livable for people. Terraforming Mars would take hundreds or even thousands of years, however.

Will these events ever happen? Will we build biosphere colonies on Mars? Will we terraform it? These are questions that the people of Earth have to answer. Some people feel strongly that Earth is just the cradle of the human race. They say that our destiny is to move out into the universe. In the long term, Mars may be just the first small step toward the stars.

Your Turn

After Reading

5. The purpose of the piece you have just read is mainly to inform. Answer these questions about information in the reading:

   A. What is a *biosphere*?
   _____
   _____

   B. What is *terraforming*?
   _____
   _____

6. List two facts that you learned from the piece.

   A. _____
   _____

   B. _____
   _____

7. Look at the third paragraph. List one opinion in that paragraph.
   _____
   _____

8. Did you think that this article was interesting and well written? Why, or why not?
   _____
   _____
   _____

162 AIM Higher! ISAT Language Arts Review

Reading Nonfiction and Fiction

Reading Fiction Actively

Fiction is just another word for stories about imaginary people and events. Here's a good approach to reading stories:

Meets ISAT Standards
1.A.1b
1.B.1a
1.B.1b
1.B.1c
1.C.1a
1.C.1b
1.C.1d
2.A.1a
2.A.1b
2.B.1a

Before Reading

Look at the title. Based on the title, do you have any idea what the story is about?

Look at the author's name. Do you know any other stories by this person? If so, what do you expect the story to be like?

Read the first couple of paragraphs of the story. **Ask yourself these questions:**

✔ What is the **setting** (the time and place of the story)?

✔ Who is the **main character** (the most important character in the story)?

✔ What is the central conflict? The **central conflict** is the biggest struggle or problem that the main character faces.

During Reading

As you read, think about what you are reading. **Use the active reading strategies:**

✔ **Ask Questions**

✔ **Visualize**

✔ **Predict**

✔ **Summarize**

✔ **Make Connections**

As you read, **pay attention to the order of events. Events** are the happenings in the story. Look for the event that ends, or resolves, the central conflict.

More ▶

Reading Skills Review 163

Reading Nonfiction and Fiction

After Reading

Think about the story by asking yourself these questions:

- ✔ In what ways did the main character change during the story?
- ✔ What did the character learn, if anything?

Based on your answers to those questions, ask yourself, What lesson, or **theme,** does the story teach?

Respond to the story by writing about it or discussing it with your friends and classmates.

Your Turn

Exercise Read the story that begins on the next page. As you read it and after you finish reading, answer the questions numbered in blue.

Meets ISAT
Standards
1.B.1a
1.B.1b
1.B.1c
1.C.1a
1.C.1b
1.C.1d
2.A.1a
2.B.1a

Before Reading the Whole Story

Read the first couple of paragraphs. Then answer these questions:

1. Who is the main character?

   _____

2. What do you know about the setting?

   _____

   _____

3. Is the main character facing some kind of big problem, or conflict? What is it?

   _____

   _____

During Reading

4. As you read the rest of the story, write down your responses. Read it actively: Question, visualize, summarize, predict, and make connections. Write at least four responses on the lines provided.

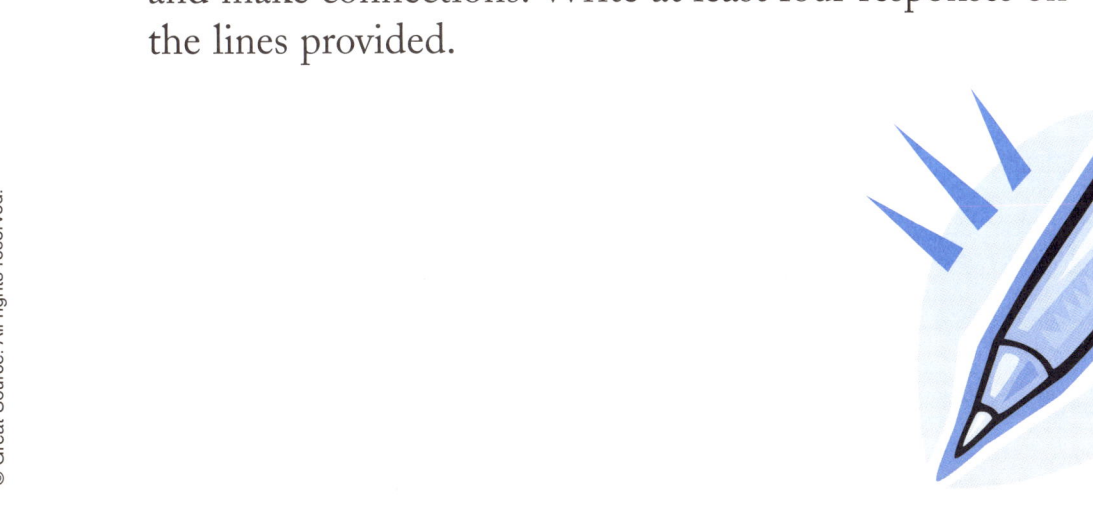

More ▶

Reading Skills Review **165**

Your Turn

Marcie's Missing Money
by Ingrid Glyph

    OK, it was a stupid thing to do, Marcie thought to herself. I should have guarded that big box of Girl Scout cookies with my life. There were twenty smaller boxes of cookies in that box. I can't believe I left them on the seat of the bus! Worse yet, the box had all the money I had collected so far in it. It was a lot of money—twenty-two dollars!

    Marcie worried all night about the money. She sent an instant message to her friend Liv to tell her about it. Liv wrote back to her, "U R in BIG trouble."

    The next morning, when the bus picked her up, Marcie spoke to the driver. "Ms. Beale, did you happen to see a box of Girl Scout cookies on the seat last night?"

    "Don't tell me you left your cookies on the seat!" Ms. Beale said.

    "Well, I think I did," answered Marcie.

    "Girl, if you did, they're long gone." Marcie's face fell.

    Immediately, Ms. Beale said, "I'm just kidding. Yes, I found your cookies on the seat." She pulled out the cardboard box stuck between her seat and the driver's side door. "Here they are. You just be more careful next time."

    "Great, Ms. Beale. Thank you!" Marcie said, feeling greatly relieved. She took the

Your Notes and Comments

box and headed back to her seat. Then she looked into the box. The cookies were all there, but the money—the twenty-two dollars—was gone. When the bus stopped, Marcie and Ms. Beale looked for the money. It was nowhere to be found.

Marcie worried about the money all day. What was she going to do? She decided to talk to her friend Cricket. When Cricket was a little girl, her dad used to call her "my little grasshopper." Her mom thought that was funny and started calling her Cricket. The nickname stuck and from then on, everyone called her Cricket, even though her real name was Stephanie.

"One thing's for sure," Cricket started to say.

"What?" said Marcie.

"You can't tell your parents," Cricket replied.

"Why not?" asked Marcie.

"Well, obviously," said Cricket, "they're going to be really, really mad."

"Yeah, maybe," said Marcie. "Then what am I going to do? I have to turn in the money two weeks from tomorrow." The thought of losing the money and keeping it a secret from her parents made Marcie feel sick in the pit of her stomach.

"What if you use your allowance?" said Cricket.

"I don't *get* an allowance," said Marcie. "Besides, it wouldn't be that much money if I did."

More ▶

Your Turn

"OK," said Cricket. "Maybe you could earn the money."

"How?" said Marcie.

"Hey. What about The Pampered Poodle?" asked Cricket.

"You mean the dog-grooming shop?" said Marcie.

"Yeah," said Cricket. "You know how it's always messy in there, with dog hair all over the floor?"

"Yeah."

"Well," said Cricket. "Why don't you ask if you could work in there a little bit after school and on the weekends? You could sweep up. That way you could earn the money."

"You know, that might work," said Marcie. "Mr. Welleck at the Pampered Poodle likes me. He always says 'hi' when Dad and I bring in Beauregarde. But I would have to get my parents' permission."

"So, get their permission. But don't tell them about the money!" Cricket said.

The next day, right after school, Marcie called Mr. Welleck at The Pampered Poodle. She asked him if he could use someone to sweep up the shop after school. Mr. Welleck agreed that he could use a little extra help in his shop. Marcie was excited about getting the job, but she explained that she would have

168 AIM Higher! ISAT Language Arts Review

to talk to her parents. Mr. Welleck told her to let him know.

That night, Marcie talked to her Dad. She asked if she could work a little bit at The Pampered Poodle. She didn't say anything about losing the money. Dad gave her about fifteen reasons why working at The Pampered Poodle would not be a good idea. He said: "First, your mom would have to drive you there and pick you up. Second, you need to do your homework at that time of day. Third, you might get bitten by one of those dogs. You know how worked up they all get when they're at the groomer's. Fourth, you need to be home to feed Beauregarde right after school...." That was the way it went.

Marcie gave up and went off to her room. Now she was REALLY worried. I have no way to get the money, she thought. Maybe people will think I stole it! Marcie clenched her fists and pounded her pillow. She had visions of a policeman showing up at her house and talking to her parents. She started crying. Then there was a knock at her door.

"Marcie, are you OK?" her father asked.

"Yes," Marcie whimpered.

"Can I come in?" Dad asked.

"OK," said Marcie.

"Do you want to tell me what this is all about?" Dad asked.

That was enough. Marcie began to sob as she told him everything.

Your Turn

When she was finished, Dad said, "Well, Marcie, losing the money was irresponsible. You should have been more careful. But you know that, don't you?" Marcie nodded. "What I'm really upset about is that you needed help and didn't tell me about this right away. That's a bigger problem. Do you understand why?"

"Yes," said Marcie. "I shouldn't have kept it a secret from you."

"OK," her dad said. "The way I see it, you have to replace the money that you lost."

"But I don't have it," Marcie said. "And you told me I couldn't work at The Pampered Poodle."

"I'll lend you the twenty-two dollars," said Dad. "But it's a loan. You're going to have to do some work around here to earn it."

"Anything," said Marcie. "Well, maybe *almost* anything." She was thinking that she really didn't want to have to clean up Beauregarde's piles from the backyard.

"I tell you what. This Saturday, you wash the windows in the house. We'll pay you fifty cents a window. So, after a few Saturdays of that, you'll be caught up."

"Forty-four windows! Do we have that many? How about a dollar a window?"

Dad, who was a businessman, admired a certain amount of wheeling and dealing. "OK. You're on," Dad said. And that's how the crisis of the missing money was solved, and that's how Marcie learned her lesson about keeping secrets from her parents.

After Reading

5. What lesson does the main character learn in this story? In other words, what is the story's theme?

_____

_____

_____

6. Would you recommend this story to a friend? Why, or why not?

_____

_____

7. Did you think that this story was interesting and well written? Why, or why not?

_____

_____

_____

Meets ISAT Standards
1.B.1a
1.B.1c
1.C.1a
1.C.1b
1.C.1d
2.B.1a

Reading Skills Review

Reading Nonfiction and Fiction

Meets ISAT Standards
1.B.1c
1.B.1d
1.B.1e

The Sounds Writers Use

Whatever kind of literature you are reading—stories, nonfiction, poetry, or plays—all have some things in common. One thing that all have in common is sound. Writers have many ways to use sound to make their work more beautiful and interesting. Here are a few:

Sounds in Literature

Rhythm. **Rhythm** is a pattern of strong or weak beats.

  Elsie Marley's grown so fine,

Rhyme. **Rhyme** is the use of the same sounds at the ends of words.

  cat, mat, pat, hat, flat, sat

  pound, sound, mound, hound, found

Onomatopoeia. **Onomatopoeia** is the use of words that sound like what they describe.

  buzz, pop, chomp, crackle, snarl, whoosh, meow, bark, clatter

Alliteration. **Alliteration** is the repetition of consonant sounds at the beginnings of words.

  Peter Piper picked a peck of pickled peppers.

Return to the questions you answered at the beginning of this unit. Check your work and fix it if necessary. Give your work to your teacher for grading.

Unit 3
Notetaking and Graphic Organizers

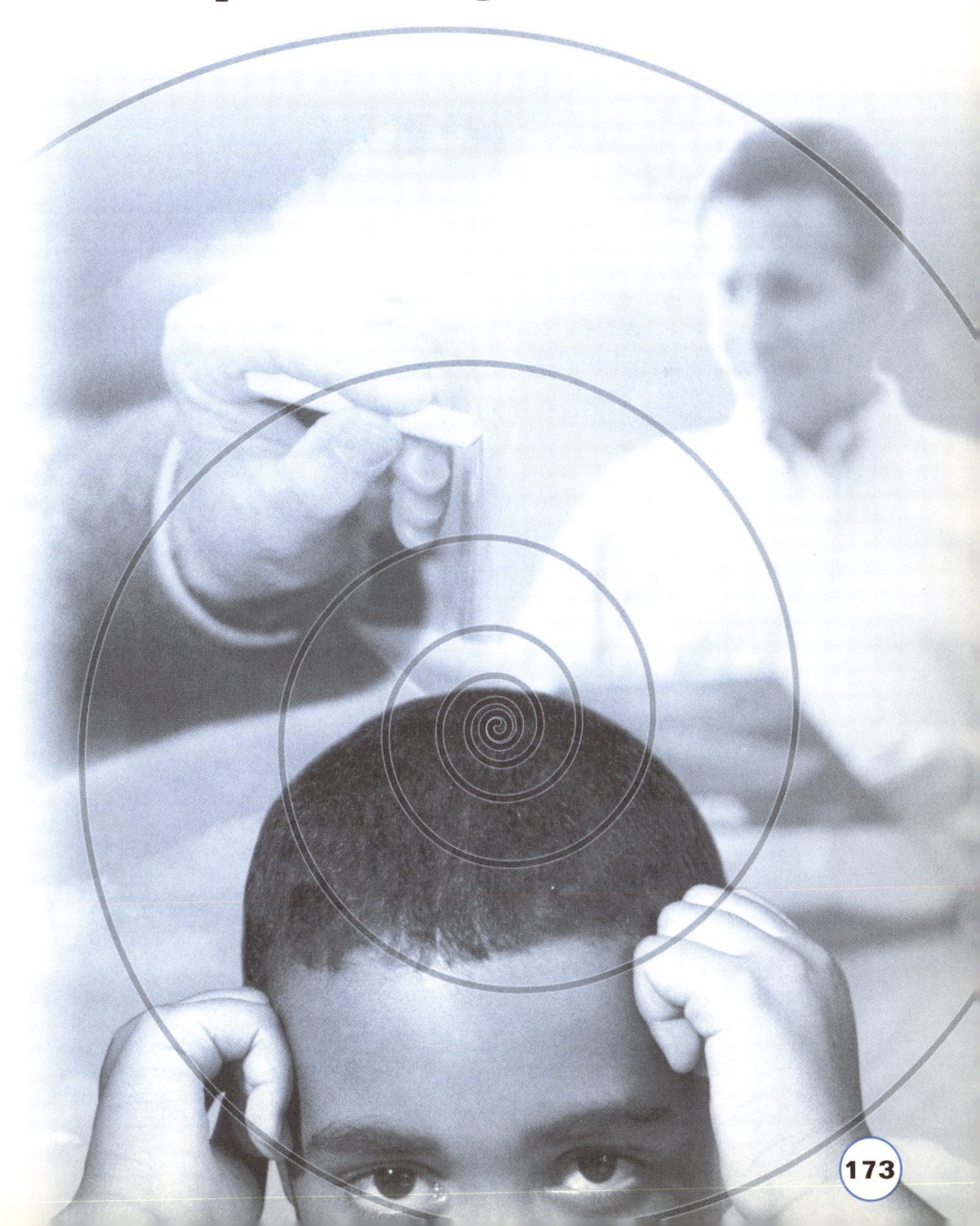

First Encounter

Read the following selection. As you read it, take notes about information that you think might be important to remember. Then use your notes to answer the questions that follow the selection. At the end of the unit, you will be asked to return to these questions to check your work and fix it if necessary.

Gators and Crocs

by Liz Sauretes

In September of 2002, Don Goodman was attacked by an alligator in Gainesville, Florida. Mr. Goodman was clearing a pond of weeds when the alligator leapt from the water and grabbed his arm. The alligator was eleven feet long from the tip of its snout to its tail. Fortunately, the alligator let go. Mr. Goodman was rushed to a hospital and survived the attack.

Land of the Big Lizards

Needless to say, people should be very careful about going into ponds, canals, and other bodies of water in southern Florida. That's because southern Florida is home to two large and dangerous lizards, the American alligator and the American crocodile. Alligators and crocodiles are also known as "gators" and "crocs." Alligators are a greater danger in Florida because there are so many of them. Scientists believe that there are about a million alligators in Florida. That's one alligator for every fifteen humans who live there! There are far fewer

Alligator/U.S. Fish and Wildlife Service

CROCODILE

American Crocodile/Everglades National Park Photo

crocodiles. The total number of crocs in Florida is probably between two hundred and six hundred.

Endangered Species

In the early 1900s, alligators and crocodiles just about disappeared in the United States. People hunted alligators and crocodiles for their tough leather hides, which were made into shoes, belts, and purses. Gators and crocs also had fewer places to live when people started to build homes, shopping malls, and golf courses near waterfronts, where gators and crocs used to live. The U.S. government put both alligators and crocodiles on their endangered species list. It became against the law to hunt and kill them. Alligators came back from near extinction and now exist in large numbers. Crocodiles have yet to make a comeback. Alligators have now been taken off the Endangered Species list. However, gators are still protected by law, because it is hard to tell gators and crocs apart. Scientists fear that people might kill crocodiles by accident, thinking that they are alligators.

How to Tell an Alligator from a Crocodile

Alligators and crocodiles are very similar. They are closely related. Both have long, heavy tails and long bodies covered with thick, leathery skin. They also have powerful jaws with sharp teeth. Both have four short legs with claws.

It is possible to tell alligators and crocodiles apart, however. Most alligators are smaller than crocodiles. Male alligators typically grow to lengths of thirteen to fourteen feet, though larger ones up to nineteen and a half feet long have been reported. Crocodiles can be even bigger. Male crocs typically grow to about sixteen feet but have been reported as large as twenty-two or

More ▶

First Encounter

twenty-three feet. Alligators have about seventy-four to eighty teeth. Crocodiles have sixty-six to sixty-eight teeth. However, most people probably will not want to get close enough to count them! From a distance, you can tell gators and crocs apart by a simple method. When an alligator closes its jaws, some of its upper teeth can be seen sticking down. When a crocodile closes its jaws, some of its bottom teeth, especially the large fourth tooth on either side, can be seen sticking up. In addition, an alligator has a broad, rounded, U-shaped snout. A crocodile, in contrast, has a more pointed, V-shaped snout.

Where to Find Alligators and Crocs

The American alligator is found throughout the southeastern United States. It can be found in Alabama, Arkansas, North and South Carolina, Florida, Georgia, Louisiana, Mississippi, Oklahoma, and Texas. Alligators live near freshwater swamps and marshes, rivers, ponds, and lakes. Especially during dry seasons, they head for any water they can find, such as drainage canals and even swimming pools or ponds on golf courses.

American crocodiles are much less common but have a wider range. They are found in swamps near the coast of southern Florida and the coasts of Central and South America. Crocodiles like both fresh water and slightly salty water found near the sea. In Florida, one group of crocodiles has been found in a cooling canal at the Turkey Point nuclear power plant.

How to Be Safe around Alligators and Crocodiles

Television programs that show people wrestling with crocodiles can be very misleading. These are very powerful and dangerous animals. It is important for you and your pets to keep your distance from them. The government of the state of Florida gives these tips for keeping safe around alligators and crocodiles. First, never try to feed one of these animals. Second, respect the animal. Do not attempt to kill, bother, or move it. Keep at least sixty feet away from it. Third, do not swim or walk near the water's edge at night, at dusk, or at dawn. Do not allow your pets near the water at these times, either. Fourth, do not swim outside of posted swimming areas. Fifth, never try to keep one of these animals as a pet.

Your Turn

Exercise A Fill in the circle next to the correct answer to each question. You may look back at the notes you took on the piece about gators and crocs.

Meets ISAT
Standards
1.B.1c
1.C.1b
1.C.1d

1. Which of the following is the main idea of the last paragraph?
   Ⓐ Crocodiles have a large tooth that sticks out.
   Ⓑ Both alligators and crocodiles are extremely dangerous.
   Ⓒ Skins of both animals were made into purses in the past.
   Ⓓ Alligators are found in Arkansas.

2. Which of the following happened FIRST?
   Ⓐ Alligators in Florida made a comeback and now number about one million.
   Ⓑ People hunted alligators and took over waterfront property where they used to live.
   Ⓒ Alligators died out in large numbers, becoming almost extinct in Florida.
   Ⓓ The U.S. government protected alligators by putting them on its Endangered Species list.

3. Which of the following happened LAST?
   Ⓐ Alligators in Florida made a comeback and now number about one million.
   Ⓑ People hunted alligators and took over waterfront property where they used to live.
   Ⓒ Alligators died out in large numbers, becoming almost extinct in Florida.
   Ⓓ The U.S. government protected alligators by putting them on its Endangered Species list.

More ▶

Notetaking and Graphic Organizers

Your Turn

4. How many alligators are there for every fifteen people living in Florida?

    Ⓐ about one

    Ⓑ about two

    Ⓒ about five

    Ⓓ about ten

5. What helped alligators to make a comeback in Florida?

    Ⓐ People hunted alligators for belts, shoes, and purses.

    Ⓑ People brought in alligators from other countries and turned them loose.

    Ⓒ The U.S. government put alligators on its Endangered Species list.

    Ⓓ Fewer people moved to Florida, so there was more room for alligators.

American Crocodile/Everglades National Park Photo

Exercise B Imagine that you work at a nature park in Florida. The park is called the Alligator Alley Nature Refuge. At your park, there are ponds and canals with alligators in them. There are also trails throughout the park. You need to put up some signs along the trails to warn visitors about alligators. On your signs, tell the visitors how they can keep themselves safe from alligators.

Use the lines below to make a rough outline of the directions you will put on the signs for visitors.

Meets ISAT Standards
1.B.1c
1.C.1d
3.B.1a
3.C.1a

MAIN IDEA: <u>Be safe around our alligators!</u>

RELATED IDEA 1: _____

RELATED IDEA 2: _____

RELATED IDEA 3: _____

RELATED IDEA 4: _____

Notetaking and Graphic Organizers 179

Chapter 7

Hold That Thought

Introduction to Notetaking

One secret to doing well in school and on tests is learning how to take notes. In this chapter, you will learn what notes are. You will also learn some ways to take notes.

What Are Notes?

Have you ever taken a telephone message for someone? If so, you probably know what notes are. A **note** is just a short reminder. Compare these examples:

How to Take Notes

Barbara,
—Dr. appt. Thurs. 3:30
—No food or drink for 4 hrs. before

How Not to Take Notes

Barbara, the doctor's office called. You have an appointment this Thursday at 3:30. The nurse said to remind you not to eat or drink for four hours before the visit.

Notice the differences between the examples. The notes in the first example are much shorter. They are not written in complete sentences. They use **abbreviations** like *Dr.* and *Thurs.* and *hrs.* for "Doctor" and "Thursday" and "hours." Notes should be short reminders that use abbreviations and phrases, not complete sentences.

When to Take Notes

You should take notes any time you have to remember something later.

You should take notes . . .
- when listening to your teacher or classmates in school.
- when reading from a textbook.
- when reading a selection during a test.

Notetaking and Graphic Organizers 181

Introduction to Notetaking

How to Take Notes

When you take notes, follow these rules:

Guidelines for Taking Notes

1. Do not try to write down everything. Look or listen for the most important ideas, and take notes on them.

2. Listen for main ideas and related, or supporting, details.

3. Do not use complete sentences. Instead, use **phrases,** or short groups of words. Make an outline:

   • Write down each main idea, beginning at the left margin.

   • Under the main ideas, write supporting details. Use a dash (—) before each supporting detail.

4. Use symbols and abbreviations. **Symbols** are marks that have special meanings, such as + for "and" or = for "equals." **Abbreviations** are shortened forms of words, such as *Amer.* for American or *1st* for first.

5. Write the date and the subject at the top of your note page.

Here is a paragraph from the piece you just read about "gators" and "crocs."

> Needless to say, people should be very careful about going into ponds, canals, and other bodies of water in southern Florida. That's because southern Florida is home to two large and dangerous lizards, the American alligator and the American crocodile. Alligators and crocodiles are also known as "gators" and "crocs." Alligators are a greater danger in Florida because there are so many of them. Scientists believe that there are about a million alligators in Florida. That's one alligator for every fifteen humans who live there! There are far fewer crocodiles. The total number of crocs in Florida is probably between two hundred and six hundred.

Here is an example of some notes a student could take on the ideas in this paragraph:

One Student's Notes (Outline)
2 large lizards in Fla.
—Amer. alligator
—Amer. crocodile
—called "gators" & "crocs"
—1 mill. gators in Fla.
—1 gator for every 15 people
—Only 200–600 crocs in Fla.

Notice that these notes are not written in sentences. These notes are written in a **rough outline.** The main idea appears first. Related ideas, or specific details, come after the most important idea. The notes use abbreviations such as *Fla.* for Florida, *Amer.* for American, *gators* for alligators, and *crocs* for crocodiles.

Meets ISAT Standards
1.B.1c
1.C.1b
5.B.1a

Introduction to Notetaking

Symbols and Abbreviations

When you take notes, you can use any symbols and abbreviations that you like. Just make sure that you will know what they mean when you look back at your notes later. Here are some common symbols and abbreviations that you can use:

Symbols	Abbreviations
= for *equals*	**ft.** for *foot*
& or **+** for *and*	**mi.** for *mile*
$ for *dollars*	**w/** for *with*
@ for *at*	**ex.** for *example*
! for *important*	**1st** for *first*
* for *important*	**U.S.** for *United States*
Δ for *change*	**def.** for *definition*

Your Turn

Exercise Below are two more paragraphs from the selection about "gators" and "crocs." Underline the topic sentence, or main idea, in each paragraph. Then, on your own paper, take notes on these two paragraphs. Use the rough outline form for taking notes that you have learned in this chapter.

Meets ISAT Standards
1.B.1c
1.C.1b
5.B.1a

Alligators and crocodiles are very similar. They are closely related. Both have long, heavy tails and long bodies covered with thick, leathery skin. They also have powerful jaws with sharp teeth. Both have four short legs with claws.

It is possible to tell alligators and crocodiles apart, however. Most alligators are smaller than crocodiles. Male alligators typically grow to lengths of thirteen to fourteen feet, though larger ones up to nineteen and a half feet long have been reported. Crocodiles can be even bigger. Male crocs typically grow to about sixteen feet but have been reported as large as twenty-two or twenty-three feet. Alligators have about seventy-four to eighty teeth. Crocodiles have sixty-six to sixty-eight. However, most people probably will not want to get close enough to count them! From a distance, you can tell gators and crocs apart by a simple method. When an alligator closes its jaws, some of its upper teeth can be seen sticking down. When a crocodile closes its jaws, some of its bottom teeth, especially the large fourth tooth on either side, can be seen sticking up. In addition, an alligator has a broad, rounded, U-shaped snout. A crocodile, in contrast, has a more pointed, V-shaped snout.

Notetaking and Graphic Organizers

Chapter 8

Picture This!

Using Graphic Organizers

In the last chapter, you learned how to take notes in a rough outline. Now you will learn some more notetaking skills. In this chapter, you will learn how to use graphic organizers for taking notes. A **graphic organizer** is a chart or a picture. Graphic organizers can be used for notetaking. They can also be used for organizing your ideas and presenting them to other people.

Making Word Webs

A **word web** is a picture that shows how ideas are connected. Read the following paragraph. Then look at the word web based on it.

Microraptor gui, which lived about 126 million years ago, was an amazing creature. It was part dinosaur and part bird. Scientists in Beijing, China, recently found several fossils of *Microraptor gui.* The creature was about three feet long. It was a member of the group of dinosaurs known as **theropods.** This group includes *Velociraptor* and *Tyrannosaurus rex.* Like these larger theropods, *Microraptor gui* had sharp teeth and claws and was a meat-eater. What makes *Microraptor gui* really interesting, however, is that it had four wings with feathers! It probably glided from tree to tree. It would have been able to spread its wings and glide down upon other animals from above.

Notice how details are clustered around the main idea at the middle of this word web.

Meets ISAT Standards
1.A.1b
1.B.1c
1.C.1b
1.C.1f
5.B.1a

- Lived 126 million years ago
- Found in Beijing, China
- Sharp claws
- Meat-eater
- Sharp teeth
- 3 ft long
- Velociraptor
- Is a theropod
- Tyrannosaurus rex
- 4 wings
  - With feathers
  - Glided
  - Used gliding to catch other animals

Microraptor gui

Notetaking and Graphic Organizers

Using Graphic Organizers

Meets ISAT
Standards
1.B.1c
1.C.1b
1.C.1f
5.B.1a

Making Timelines

A **timeline** shows a series of events and the dates when they happened. From a timeline, you can see at a glance the order in which things happened. Read this paragraph. Then look at the timeline based on it.

Photo: Dr. George Washington Carver; Library of Congress, Prints & Photographs Division [LC-USW3-000165-D].

George Washington Carver was born around 1864, on a plantation in Missouri. When the Civil War ended in 1865, many former slaves became farmers on small plots of land. Carver worked on a farm when he was a teenager. He grew up to become a famous horticulturalist—a person who studies plants. He got a master's degree from Iowa State University in 1896. That same year, he took a job as a professor and researcher at the Tuskegee Institute in Alabama. Carver dedicated his life to helping southern farmers. He taught them how to grow more and better crops on the same land by changing the crops that they grew from year to year. Between 1896 and the year that he died, 1943, he developed over three hundred uses for peanuts and one hundred uses for sweet potatoes. This made it possible for poor southern farmers to sell their crops more easily and for more money. In 1947 and 1998, Carver was honored by having his picture placed on postage stamps. He was elected to the National Inventor's Hall of Fame in 1990. In 1994, fifty-one years after his death, Carver was also honored by Iowa State University. They awarded him a special degree called a doctor of humane letters.

Notice how easy it is to compare the dates of these events by looking at them on a timeline.

George Washington Carver (1864–1943)

- Civil War ends (1865)
- Carver develops 300 uses for peanuts; 100 uses for sweet potatoes
- Carver's picture placed on postage stamp (1947)
- Carver elected to Inventor's Hall of Fame (1990)
- Carver's picture placed on postage stamp (1998)

1860 | 1870 | 1880 | 1890 | 1900 | 1910 | 1920 | 1930 | 1940 | 1950 | 1960 | 1970 | 1980 | 1990 | 2000

- Carver born (1864)
- Carver gets master's degree; takes job at Tuskegee Institute (1896)
- Carver dies (1943)
- Carver receives doctor of humane letters degree (1994)

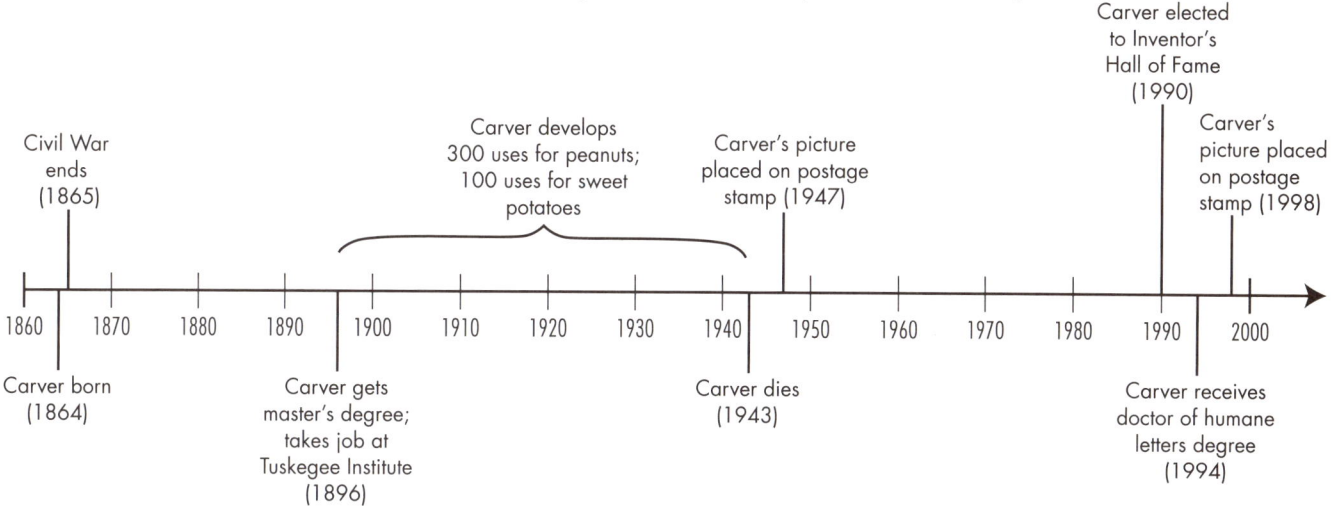

◀ **Here is a picture of Carver's students at work growing plants in a greenhouse.**

Photos, top to bottom: Tuskegee Institute, Alabama, Students in the greenhouse [LC-USW3-000185-D]; Tuskegee Institute, ca. 1918 [LC-USZ62-128399]; Dr. George Washington Carver talks to members of the Reserve Officers Training Corps [LC-USW3-000167-D]. Library of Congress, Prints & Photographs Division.

Carver (seated in this photo) ▶ taught at Tuskegee Institute in Alabama.

Notetaking and Graphic Organizers

Using Graphic Organizers

Meets ISAT
Standards
1.B.1c
1.C.1b
1.C.1f
5.B.1a

Making Charts

A **chart** presents information in rows (running across the page) and columns (running up and down the page). Read the following paragraph. Then look at the chart that one student made based on it.

Brains and computers are similar in some ways and different in others. Both the brain and a computer take in information (inputs) and give out information (outputs). Both process information, or change it around to achieve some purpose. Both can store, or keep, information for a short time or for a long time. Both are divided into many parts that do different tasks. Both brains and computers run programs to do particular tasks. For example, they might both run a program for recognizing the letter A. Brains differ from computers in some ways, too. Brains are slower, but they can do a lot more tasks that computers can. Brains are capable of feeling and being aware of themselves, of others, and of the world around them. Computers are not. Some people believe that eventually, computers will be able to do everything that brains can do. Other people believe that that will never happen.

190 **AIM Higher! ISAT Language Arts Review**

Brains and Computers

Similarities	Differences
Both take in information (inputs).	Brains are slower.
Both give out information (outputs).	Brains can do more.
Both process information.	Computers are faster.
Both store information.	Computers have no feelings.
Both are divided into many parts.	Computers are not aware of themselves, of others, and of the world.
Both run programs.	

Notetaking and Graphic Organizers

Using Graphic Organizers

Using Graphic Organizers for Notetaking

Usually, when you take notes, you should use the rough outline form. You learned how to make a rough outline in the last chapter. Sometimes, however, you may want to include a graphic organizer in your notes. For example, suppose that you are taking notes in class. Your teacher is telling the class about the Civil War. When the teacher starts mentioning dates, you might make a quick timeline in your notes.

Here is another example: Suppose that you are taking notes on a chapter that you are reading in your science textbook. You come to a place where the textbook is comparing and contrasting plants and animals. You might make a quick chart in your notes. You could list the similarities in one column and the differences in another, as shown on the previous page.

Your Turn

Exercise A Read this paragraph. As you read the paragraph, take notes by creating a word web. (Hint: The words WHALE SHARK should appear at the center of your web.)

Meets ISAT Standards
1.B.1c
5.B.1a

Whale sharks are the gentle giants of the sea. Up to fifty feet long, the whale shark is the largest of all fish. It is longer than a school bus! One of these fish can weigh more than 27,000 pounds. That's more than thirteen tons! The whale shark is dark gray to reddish or greenish brown on its back and sides. The underside of the fish is white or whitish yellow. The top side of the fish is a dark color with white or whitish yellow spots. Despite its enormous size, the whale shark is quite gentle. It lives on tiny creatures in the sea known as plankton as well as on small fish and squid. The whale shark swallows huge mouthfuls of water and plankton or fish, but it does not eat people. Divers can approach the whale shark without fear.

Exercise B Read this paragraph. As you read the paragraph, take notes on it by creating a timeline.

Kalpana Chawla was born in 1961 in Karnal, India. She grew up to become an astronaut. She was one of the great heroes of the American space program. As a girl, she became interested in space flight. After graduating from college in India in 1982, she came to the United States. She did more advanced studies at the University of Texas at Arlington and at the University of Colorado. Then, in 1994, NASA selected her for its astronaut training program. In 1998 she flew her first shuttle mission. She made 252 orbits of the Earth and traveled 6.5 million miles. She spent more than 376 hours in space. Then, in 2003, she flew her second shuttle mission. This was a sixteen-day scientific mission aboard the space shuttle *Columbia*. Tragically, the *Columbia* blew up as it returned to the Earth's atmosphere. Ms. Chawla became one of seven heroes lost in this terrible tragedy.

Notetaking and Graphic Organizers

Your Turn

Meets ISAT Standards
1.C.1f
3.B.1b
3.C.1a

Exercise C The following chart describes similarities and differences between cats and dogs. Use the information in the chart to write a paragraph about those similarities and differences. Write the paragraph on your own paper. Begin with a topic sentence that says that there are both similarities and differences between dogs and cats. Then use details from the chart to complete your paragraph.

Similarities	Differences
Both have fur.	Cats are independent. Dogs are not.
Both have teeth and claws.	Dogs are easily trained. Cats are not.
Both are pets.	Dogs often do work for people. Cats do not.
Both can be housebroken.	

Return to the questions you answered at the beginning of this unit. Check your work and fix it if necessary. Give your work to your teacher for grading.

AIM Higher! ISAT Language Arts Review

Unit 4
Writing Skills Review

First Encounter

Read the following writing prompt. Next, read the rough outline and final draft that one student created in response to the prompt. Then answer the questions that follow these examples.

A **writing prompt** is a set of directions. These directions tell a student what to write.

Writing Prompt

Think about a time when something happened in your life that taught you an important lesson. Write a paragraph to tell the story of what happened. Make sure to tell what you learned from the experience.

Here is the outline one student made in response to this prompt:

One Student's Rough Outline

What I learned: It's fun to watch nature in action
—Got package of Sea-Monkeys® as gift
—Sea-Monkeys® are tiny brine shrimp
—Put bottled water in Sea-Monkey® aquarium
—Added packet to make water pure enough
—Waited 24 hours
—Added "instant life" packet → watched Sea-Monkeys® hatch
—Enjoyed watching Sea-Monkeys® grow

196 AIM Higher! ISAT LANGUAGE ARTS REVIEW

Here is the final draft that the student wrote in response to the prompt.

One Student's Final Draft

Kai Shulka

A Little World

A little package that I received as a birthday gift taught me how much fun it can be to watch nature in action. For my ninth birthday, my Aunt Karen bought me a Sea-Monkey® kit. Inside the kit was a plastic fishbowl, an instruction book, and three packets—one to keep the water clear, one with the Sea-Monkey® eggs, and one for their food. First, I filled the aquarium with bottled water. Then I poured in the packet to make the water pure and waited for 24 hours. Once the water was pure, I was ready to hatch my Sea-Monkeys.® I poured in the contents of the Instant Life packet. The Sea-Monkeys® hatched right away and started swimming around! They were so tiny that I had to hold the aquarium up to a light to see them. Sea-Monkeys® are actually a kind of shrimp called brine shrimp. It was a lot of fun to see my Sea-Monkeys® grow and swim around. It was truly a miracle to see them burst into life.

Your Turn

Exercise A Answer the following questions about the writing prompt and the student's response. Remember to write in complete sentences.

1. Look at the writing prompt again. What does the prompt ask the student to write about?

   _____
   _____
   _____

2. What did the student do before writing his response?

   _____
   _____

3. Do you think that doing this was helpful? Why or why not?

   _____
   _____
   _____

4. Do you think the student will get a good score for his response? Why or why not?

   _____
   _____
   _____
   _____

Exercise B Write your own response to the writing prompt on page 196. First, make a rough outline. Then write your first draft on your own paper. Revise and proofread your draft, using the checklists on pages 211 and 213. Then copy your final draft onto the lines below.

Meets ISAT
Standards
1.B.1c
3.A.1
3.B.1a
3.B.1b
3.C.1a

Chapter 9

Step by Step

The Writing Process

Do you like to draw or paint? Do you like to build or model with clay? Creating things can be lots of fun. Like drawing, painting, building, or modeling, writing can be a chance for you to create. By writing, you can make things that did not exist before—stories, poems, and essays, for example. Writing can also be a way for you to share what you care about with other people.

Writing is a process. A process is anything that takes place over time, not all at once. A **process** usually involves a series of steps. So, for example, getting ready for a vacation is a process. So is learning how to ride a bike. A process is not something that happens in a flash, like a shooting star. It is something that takes time.

The **writing process** is made up of several steps. This chart shows the steps in the writing process:

Meets ISAT Standards
1.B.1c
3.A.1
3.B.1a
3.B.1b
3.C.1a

Steps in the Writing Process

1 Prewriting   During this step, you choose a topic. You think about who your readers will be. You come up with a main idea. You gather information. You organize your information, or put it in an order that makes sense.

2 Drafting   During this step, you get your ideas down on paper.

3 Evaluating and Revising   During this step, you study what you've written. You look for ways to improve it by putting information in a different order, adding more specific words or details to show or explain what you mean, and so on. You rewrite what you've done, making it better.

4 Proofreading   During this step, you check for errors in spelling, grammar, usage, punctuation, and capitalization.

5 Publishing   The final step in the process is to share your work with others.

Writing Skills Review 201

The Writing Process

Prewriting

Let's look at one student's writing process, step by step. Marcie took a writing test. The test had a writing prompt. A **writing prompt** is a set of directions that tell you what to write. Here is the writing prompt from Marcie's test:

> **Writing Prompt**
>
> Almost all young people love animals. Choose some animal that you know well or have watched or taken care of. Write a paragraph describing that animal. Imagine that the paragraph will be posted on a bulletin board to be read by other students in your school.

Study the Writing Prompt

Marcie first studied the writing prompt carefully. Doing so helped her to plan her piece of writing. By looking at the prompt, Marcie learned a lot about the piece of writing she was supposed to do. She took these notes:

> **One Student's Notes**
>
> Subject: an animal I know well or have some experience with
> Purpose: to describe
> Type of writing: a paragraph
> Readers: other students in my school

Come up with a Narrowed Topic

A **topic** is something you will write about. Sometimes, the topic is given to you. At other times, you might be given a general subject, and you have to come up with a specific topic related to that subject. The writing prompt at the beginning of this lesson tells Marcie to write about an animal. This is a very general subject. Now Marcie has to come up with a more specific topic to write about. When you **narrow** a subject, you make it more specific. Here are Marcie's notes on some possible narrowed topics:

> Subject: an animal I know well or have some experience with
> Possible narrowed topics: dogs (beagle), birds (parakeet), zoo animals (giraffe, cobra, wolf)

Marcie has a pet beagle. She decided to write about her beagle because she knew a lot about him.

State Your Main Idea

The main idea of a piece of writing is what the piece is mostly about. After deciding on a topic, Marcie came up with this sentence that states her main idea:

> My beagle Beauregarde is my best friend.

Meets ISAT Standards
1.B.1c
3.B.1a
3.B.1b

Your Turn

Exercise A For each subject below, write two topics that are more narrow.

EXAMPLE
GENERAL SUBJECT: Special effects in movies

NARROWED TOPIC 1: The making of Gollum in Lord of the Rings

NARROWED TOPIC 2: Special effects in the movie Spiderman

1. General subject: Sports

   Narrowed topic 1: _____

   Narrowed topic 2: _____

2. General subject: School

   Narrowed topic 1: _____

   Narrowed topic 2: _____

3. General subject: Animals

   Narrowed topic 1: _____

   Narrowed topic 2: _____

Exercise B Choose one of your narrowed topics from the exercise above. Write one sentence that states your main idea for a paragraph on this topic.

MY MAIN IDEA: _____

_____

_____

The Writing Process

Gather Information

The next step in prewriting is to gather information about your topic. There are many ways to do this. Here are some common ways to gather information:

Meets ISAT Standards
1.B.1c
3.B.1a
3.B.1b
5.B.1a

How to Gather Information for a Piece of Writing

- Make a list
- Make a chart
- Make a word web
- Interview people
- Look in books, magazines, newspapers, and on the Internet

To gather information for her paragraph, Marcie decided to make a list of sensory details about her dog. **Sensory details** are details about sight, sound, touch, taste, and smell.

<u>Beauregarde the Beagle</u>

Sight
—Wags his tail really fast & shakes all over
—White with black & brown places
—Big brown eyes
—Big for a beagle
—Lies on couch

Sound
—Barks at other dogs thru the window
—Whimpers when you rub his belly

More ▶

Writing Skills Review **205**

The Writing Process

Touch
—Loves to snuggle
—Has a wet nose
—Loves to play tug of war
Taste
—Wolfs down his food
Smell
—Has great sense of smell—
  follows his nose

Organize Your Ideas

The next step in prewriting is to **organize** your ideas. This means putting your ideas in an order that makes sense. Here are some common ways to organize ideas:

Ways to Organize Ideas

Time Order. Put the ideas in the order in which they happen, from first to last.

Spatial Order. Put the ideas in the order in which you see them. For example, you can list details from top to bottom, from left to right, or from front to back.

Order of Importance. Put the ideas in order of importance—from most important to least important or from least important to most important.

Marcie decided to organize her ideas in time order. She decided to tell about a typical day in Beauregarde's life. Marcie rearranged the notes from her list to make this rough outline:

Meets ISAT Standards
1.B.1c
3.B.1a
3.B.1b
5.B.1a

One Student's Rough Outline

Morning
—Waits at door
—Big brown eyes
—Big for a beagle—body like a basset hound
—Whimpers when I rub his belly
—Comes downstairs w/me
—Wolfs down his food

During day
—Lies on couch or in sunlight

Evening
—Meets me at door when I come home from school
—Wags tail really fast & shakes all over
—Loves to play tug of war
—Loves to snuggle
—Sometimes barks at other dogs thru window

Writing Skills Review 207

Your Turn

Exercise A The following is a list of details for a paragraph about the artist Joan Miró. Use the dates (years) to put the details in time order. Number the details to show the order in which they should appear. The first one has been done for you.

____ Was given degree from the University of Barcelona, 1979

____ In 1960s, created a lot of large art for public places

__1__ Born in Barcelona, 1893

____ Died in Palma de Mallorca in 1983

____ In 1921, showed his work in a gallery in Paris

____ Had his first showing of his work in Barcelona in 1918

____ In 1930s–1950s, became one of the great artists of the 20th century

Exercise B The following is a list of details for a paragraph about a scene at a beach. Organize the details in spatial order, beginning with the land and heading out to sea. Number the details to show the order in which they should appear.

____ People windsurfing & swimming

____ A lighthouse & a boathouse

____ Sailboats on the horizon

____ Waves breaking on the sand & shorebirds running along the water's edge

____ People in brightly colored bathing suits, lying on the sand

AIM Higher! ISAT Language Arts Review

The Writing Process

Drafting

After you have finished planning a piece of writing, you are ready to begin drafting. **Drafting** is the process of getting your ideas down on paper. Simply follow the rough outline that you made to organize your notes. Here is the draft that Marcie made based on her outline:

Meets ISAT Standards
1.B.1c
3.B.1a
3.B.1b
5.B.1a

One Student's Rough Draft

My beagle Beauregarde is my best friend. In the morning when I wake up, he is always waiting for me. I open up, and their he is. He has big brown eyes. And a long body like a basset hound. The minute he sees me, he rolls over on his belly. For a tummy rub. Then he comes downstairs. I feed him, he wolfs down his food. He lies around on the couch during the day. Or in a patch of sunlight near a window. I get home from school and he meets me at the door. Wagging his tail really fast and shakeing all over. At night we play tug of war with a sock, sometimes we snuggle on the sofa. Hes always very well behaved. Not when he sees another dog, tho—then he howls like crazy! Oh, and when I rub his tummy, he closes his eyes and wimpers.

Writing Skills Review **209**

The Writing Process

Meets ISAT Standards
1.B.1c
3.A.1
3.B.1a
3.B.1b
3.C.1a

Revising

Revising is a two-step process. First, you **evaluate,** or judge, your writing. That is, you look it over to see how it can be improved. Then, you can edit what you have written or start all over again. When you **edit** your work, you can make corrections like these:

- You can add material.   Jack and Jill fell down. *(insert: the hill)*

- You can move material.   Jack and Jill fell ~~down~~.

- You can cut material.   Jack ⟨and⟩ Jill fell down.

- You can change material.   Jack and Jill fell down ~~the hill~~. *(insert: but did not get hurt)*

The checklist on the next page tells what to look for when you are evaluating your own writing.

AIM Higher! ISAT Language Arts Review

© Great Source. All rights reserved.

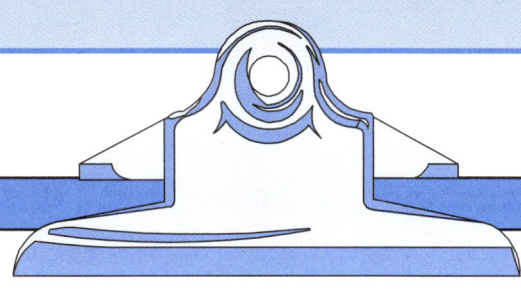

Revision Checklist

✔ **Think about Your Readers**
- ❏ Is the piece of writing right for your readers? Will they understand it?
- ❏ Do you need to give them more or less information?

✔ **Think about the Purpose**
- ❏ If you are writing for a test, does your writing answer the test prompt (question) completely?
- ❏ Does the writing do what it is supposed to do? Does it persuade, inform, describe, or entertain?

✔ **Check the Style and Voice**
- ❏ Are the words that you used the right ones for the job? Can you think of other words that are more precise or concrete or more interesting?
- ❏ Is the writing interesting to read?

✔ **Check the Structure and Organization**
- ❏ Does each paragraph have a main idea?
- ❏ Did you include all the important details?
- ❏ Are the ideas in an order that makes sense?
- ❏ Are the connections between ideas clear?

✔ **Check the Focus and Supporting Details**
- ❏ Does every sentence in each paragraph support the topic sentence?
- ❏ Are there any sentences that do not belong?
- ❏ Are there enough details to support the topic sentence?

The Writing Process

Here is the revised version of Marcie's paragraph about her dog. Notice that although she has improved it, she still needs to proofread it and fix a few more mistakes.

One Student's Revised Paragraph

My beagle Beauregarde is my best friend. In the morning when I wake up, he is always waiting for me. I open ~~up~~ my eyes, and ~~their he is.~~ ~~He has~~ with his big brown eyes. ~~And~~ He has a long body like a basset hound. The minute he sees me, ~~he~~ Beau rolls over on his back ~~belly.~~ For a tummy rub. Then he comes downstairs, and I feed him, as if he might not ever be fed again. To work off the big meal, he wolfs down his food. He lies around on the couch ~~during~~ all ~~the~~ day. ~~Or~~ In the winter, he might lie in a patch of sunlight near a window. When I get home from school ~~and~~, he meets me at the door. Wagging his tail really fast and shaking all over. At night we play tug of war with a sock, sometimes we snuggle on the sofa. Hes always very well behaved. Not when he sees another dog, tho — At those times ~~then~~ a coyote he howls like crazy! ~~Oh, and~~ when I rub his tummy, he closes his eyes and wimpers.

Proofreading

After revising your work, the next step is to make a clean copy and then to proofread it. When you **proofread,** you check for errors in spelling, grammar, usage, punctuation, and capitalization. Then you correct your mistakes neatly, using marks like the ones shown on the next page. This chart shows what to look for when you are proofreading:

Meets ISAT Standards
1.B.1c
3.A.1
3.B.1b
3.C.1a

Proofreading Checklist

✔ **Form**
- ❏ The first line of every paragraph is indented.
- ❏ There are margins on both sides of the paper.
- ❏ The handwriting is clear.

✔ **Grammar and Usage**
- ❏ Each sentence is a complete thought.
- ❏ Each sentence has a subject (noun) and a predicate (verb).
- ❏ There are no run-on sentences. Two or more sentences are not jammed together as one.

✔ **Spelling**
- ❏ All words, including names, are spelled correctly.

✔ **Capitalization**
- ❏ Every sentence begins with a capital letter.
- ❏ All names of specific people and places begin with a capital letter.

✔ **Punctuation**
- ❏ Every sentence has an end mark—a period (.), an exclamation point (!), or a question mark (?).
- ❏ Commas are used correctly.
- ❏ All words quoted from other people (including other writers) are in quotation marks.

Writing Skills Review

The Writing Process

When you proofread, make your corrections as neatly as possible. For example, do not scratch out a word and scribble a replacement above it. Instead, draw a single line through the word you want to replace. Then write in the new word neatly above it. Here are some proofreading symbols that will be useful to you:

Revision and Proofreading Symbols

Symbol	Example	Meaning
∧	a red ∧ bike (*mountain*)	Add something that is missing here.
℘	a ~~really~~ hard problem	Take out letters or words here.
∾	a wi∾erd sound	Switch the order of letters or words.
⌒	some ⌒ thing great	Close up space here.
#	panda#bear	Add a space here.
/	the harvest M/oon	Make this letter lowercase.
≡	President a≡dams	Capitalize this.
¶	storm.¶ Later,	Begin a new paragraph here.
⊙	Step this way⊙	Add a period here.
∧,	boats, cars∧, and planes	Add a comma here.
∧	a ~~dum~~ ∧ idea (*dumb*)	Change this crossed-out word or phrase; correct a spelling

214 AIM Higher! ISAT LANGUAGE ARTS REVIEW

Here is a copy of Marcie's proofread paragraph:

One Student's Proofread Paragraph

 My beagle Beauregarde is my best friend. In the morning when I wake up, he is always waiting for me. I open my eyes, and there he is, with his big brown eyes. He has a long body like a basset hound. The minute he sees me, Beau rolls over on his back. For a tummy rub. When I rub his tummy, he closes his eyes and whimpers. Then he comes downstairs and I feed him. He wolfs down his food as if he might not ever be fed again. To work off the big meal, he lies around on the couch all day. In the winter, he might lie in a patch of sunlight near a window. When I get home from school, he meets me at the door, wagging his tail really fast and shaking all over. At night we play tug of war with a sock, sometimes we snuggle on the sofa. He's always very well behaved, except when he sees another dog. At those times, he howls like a crazy coyote!

Your Turn

Exercise A Rewrite the following sentences. Make all the corrections shown by the proofreading marks. (If you don't remember what the symbols mean, look back at the chart on page 214.)

1. Beleive it or not, fish do not have eyelids.

2. striped bass are called stripers in massachusetts and rockfish in maryland

3. tunas and some sharks can swim as fast as 50 mph.

4. many fish are named after other animals examples include the searobin the pigfish the porcupinefish and the leopard toadfish

5. Fish scales are used to make some lip stick and nail polish shiny

216 AIM Higher! ISAT Language Arts Review

Exercise B *The following paragraph has some errors in it. These errors are listed below. Use proofreading marks to fix the errors.*

Meets ISAT Standards
1.B.1c
3.A.1

Snails, clams, and some other soft bodied creatures without back bones are mollusks. Some, such as clams and oysters, have shells. Others, such as squid and octopuss, do not. Some mollusks grow to be real big. the giant clam can wiegh as much as 500 lbs. But that's nothing like the size of the giant squid? This mysterious creatures grows to over sixty feet in length!

Make the proofreading changes described below. Use proofreading marks to make these changes.

1. Add a hyphen (-) between the words *soft* and *bodied* in the first sentence. (*Soft* describes the *body* of these creatures.)
2. Join together the words *back* and *bones* in the first sentence.
3. Add an *e* between the two *s*'s in the word *octopuss* in the third sentence.
4. Change the word *real* to *really* in the next sentence.
5. Use a capital letter to begin the word *the* at the beginning of the next sentence.
6. Switch the *i* and the *e* in the word *wiegh*.
7. Change the abbreviation *lbs.* to the word *pounds* and add a comma.
8. In the next sentence, change the capital *B* in *But* to lowercase.
9. Change the question mark after *giant squid* to a period.
10. Cut the *s* at the end of the word *creatures* in the last sentence.

Writing Skills Review **217**

The Writing Process

Publishing or Sharing

The last step in the writing process is the easiest. In this step, you share your work with other people. Here are some of the many ways in which you can share your writing:

Publishing or Sharing Written Work
- Put it on a bulletin board.
- Make a booklet or scrapbook to show to others.
- Read your work aloud.
- Show your work to a friend, classmate, teacher, or relative.
- Send your work to a newspaper.
- Enter your work in a contest.

You have now seen all the steps in the writing process. Keep in mind these parts of the process when taking written tests:

How to Write Answers for Tests
- **Prewriting:** Read the prompt carefully. Choose a topic and narrow it down. Gather ideas. Then put your ideas in order in a rough outline.
- **Drafting:** Use your outline to write a first draft. Do not worry too much about making mistakes at this point. Follow the order in your outline.
- **Evaluating and Revising:** Reread your draft. Look for places where you might add, remove, move, or change words, phrases, or sentences to make your writing better.
- **Proofreading and Correcting:** Read your response one more time. Fix any mistakes you missed in spelling, punctuation, capitalization, grammar, and choice of words.

Chapter 10

Perfect Paragraphs

Main Ideas and Supporting Details

Knowing how to put together a paragraph well is one of the secrets to good writing. In this chapter, you will learn this secret.

What Is a Paragraph?

A **paragraph** is a group of sentences about a single main idea. Read this paragraph about how to keep fish healthy in an aquarium.

Meets ISAT Standards
1.B.1c
1.B.1d
1.C.1b
3.A.1
3.B.1a
3.B.1b
3.C.1a
3.C.1b
4.B.1a

topic sentence

Some simple steps will help make sure that the fish in your aquarium are healthy. First, make sure to change part of the water about every other week. Second, make sure to treat tap water with conditioner before adding it to your tank. Third, do not overfeed your fish. Give them only what they can eat in three to five minutes. Fourth, never clean your tank with soap. Fifth, keep your filter clean, and make sure that it is working well. Sixth, do not overfill your tank with fish. If you have six fish, each one inch long, they need six gallons of water. Seventh, do not add water from a fish store to your tank. Eighth, check the water temperature in your tank to make sure it is not too hot or too cold. If you take all these steps, you will avoid most of the mistakes people make if they are new to keeping fish.

supporting ideas

clincher sentence

Writing Skills Review

Main Ideas and Supporting Details

Notice that the paragraph you just read has the following parts:

- The first sentence (in blue) is the **topic sentence.** It tells the main idea of the paragraph.

- The last sentence (also in blue) is the **clincher sentence,** or the **concluding sentence.** It restates the main idea in different words.

- The sentences between the topic sentence and the clincher sentence are **supporting sentences.** These sentences give details that support the main idea in the topic sentence. When you **support** an idea, you show or explain what you mean by giving details or examples.

- The words *first, second, third,* and so on are **transitions.** They connect the ideas in the paragraph.

A paragraph is like a peanut butter and banana sandwich. The topic sentence is the slice of bread on top. The supporting sentences are all the filling in the middle. When you choose the details that go in the middle, you can add flavor to your writing as you explain your main idea. The clincher sentence is the slice of bread on the bottom. It completes the package of related ideas in your paragraph.

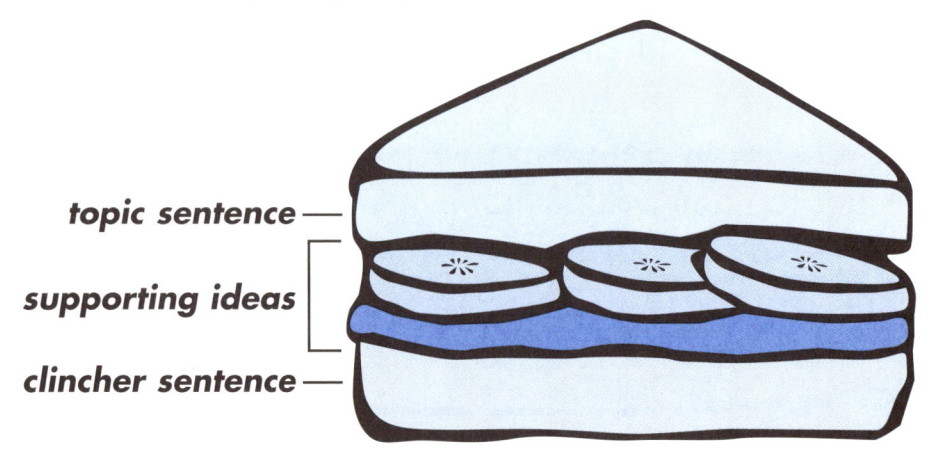

topic sentence

supporting ideas

clincher sentence

Here is a list of useful words and phrases you can use to connect ideas within a paragraph.

Meets ISAT Standards
1.B.1c
3.B.1a
3.B.1b

> **Transitions, or Words That Connect Ideas**
>
> **Words that show how things are related in time:**
> first, second, next, then, later, before, after
>
> **Words that show how things are related in place:**
> next to, above, beyond, in the back, in the front, on top, around, behind, across
>
> **Words that show connections between causes and effects or between reasons and conclusions:**
> as a result, therefore, consequently, because, since, in summary, in short
>
> **Words that show contrast between opposite ideas:**
> in contrast, unlike, on the other hand, but, however, instead
>
> **Words that show comparison between similar ideas:**
> another, similarly, in comparison
>
> **Words that lead in to examples or show that another example is next:**
> for example, for instance, one kind, also, in addition, another, one other, another kind, another type

In the next chapter, you will see how you can also use some of these words to show how your ideas are related when you are writing a paper or essay that is more than one paragraph long.

Writing Skills Review 221

Main Ideas and Supporting Details

Types of Paragraph

In the previous section of this chapter, you learned how to write a paragraph in standard form. A **standard paragraph** has a topic sentence, supporting sentences, and a clincher sentence. The **topic sentence**—the one that tells the main idea—often comes first in a paragraph. As you read different kinds of writing, you will see that some paragraphs do not follow this form. Here are some ways in which paragraphs might be different:

1. In some paragraphs, the topic sentence may appear at the end or somewhere in the middle instead of at the beginning.

2. Some paragraphs have no topic sentence at all. This is often true, for example, of paragraphs in stories.

3. Some paragraphs do not have a clincher sentence.

Your Turn

Exercise A Read these paragraphs. Underline the topic sentence in each paragraph. Remember that the topic sentence does not always come first in the paragraph.

Meets ISAT Standards
1.B.1c
1.C.1b
3.B.1a
3.B.1b

1. Many varieties of American music were created by African Americans. Before the Civil War, African Americans created the kind of music known as spirituals. After the Civil War, African Americans in the South created the type of music known as the blues. The blues led to many other varieties of music, including ragtime, jazz, soul, R&B, rock 'n' roll, and rap and hip-hop. Truly, music in America owes a great debt to African American musicians.

2. Nature uses the same forms over and over. Consider, for example, the way branches form on a tree. The same form appears in the branches of a river. It also appears in the branches of the veins and nerves in your body. You can even see the same kind of branching in the crystals of ice that form on a window.

3. Have you ever thought much about ants? If you watch ants carefully, you will see that they have some very interesting and unusual behavior. Some ants make war on other ant colonies. Some take prisoners and make them work as slaves. Other ants farm, growing mushrooms as crops. Some ants keep herds of little insects called aphids and "milk" them for a sweet food called honeydew.

Your Turn

Exercise B Read the following paragraph. Underline the topic sentence once. Then, underline the clincher sentence twice. Finally, circle the transitions the writer used to connect ideas.

When buying a fish tank, you can choose between a glass one or a plastic one. Each type of fish tank has some advantages and disadvantages. Glass tanks are cheap and they are hard to scratch. However, they can be quite heavy, and they are also easy to break. Plastic tanks, on the other hand, do not break easily and are light to carry. However, they scratch easily and are usually more expensive than glass. So, when buying a tank, you have to weigh these advantages and disadvantages to decide which kind of tank is best for you and your fish.

Exercise C *Choose a word or phrase (group of words) from the chart on page 221 to connect the ideas in the sentences below. More than one of the transitions listed in the chart could be used in each sentence. Choose the one that you think works best.*

Meets ISAT Standards
1.B.1c
3.B.1b

1. My brother is a very good performer. _____, I am not.

2. Each summer, some of the children in our town put on a play. My brother always gets a leading role. _____, he was Oliver in the play *Oliver,* and he was Tom in *The Adventures of Tom Sawyer.*

3. I always get a less important role. My part usually does not have many lines _____ I have a hard time memorizing them.

4. My brother has some good tricks for memorizing his lines. _____, he separates the play into scenes. _____, he reads the each scene to himself until he thinks he knows his lines. _____, he practices saying the lines without the script. He has someone else (like me) hold the script and tell him any lines he forgets.

5. Actors have to be able to read well and have a good memory. _____, if you want to become a good actor, read a lot and practice memorizing what you read.

Writing Skills Review **225**

Main Ideas and Supporting Details

Writing Paragraphs for Tests

Sometimes you will need to write a paragraph to answer a test question. Follow these steps:

Step 1: Read the question carefully. Make sure that you understand what the question or writing prompt is asking you to do.

Step 2: Write one sentence that is a short answer to the question or prompt. This sentence will become the topic sentence of your paragraph.

Step 3: Add some details to support the main idea in your topic sentence. Make a list of the supporting details you will include in your answer before you write it.

Step 4: Indent the first line of your topic sentence. Then write out your supporting ideas.

Step 5: Use words and phrases called **transitions** to connect your ideas. Transitions include words and phrases like *first, then, next, however, as a result,* and *for example.* (See the chart on page 221 for a more complete list.)

Step 6: Write a clincher (concluding) sentence. The clincher sentence can state your main idea again in different words.

Step 7: Look over your paragraph carefully. Ask yourself these questions:

- ✔ Did I indent the first line?
- ✔ Did I spell all my words correctly?
- ✔ Did I use a capital letter at the beginning of each sentence?
- ✔ Did I use a capital letter at the beginning of each name of a person or place?
- ✔ Did I use a period, question mark, or exclamation point at the end of each sentence?

Your Turn

Exercise A Choose one of the following topics or one of your own. Do some research on your topic. You can do this research on the Internet or use books and magazines in a library. Then, come up with a more focused (narrowed) topic. Write your narrowed topic and a topic sentence that tells your main idea on the lines provided below.

Meets ISAT
Standards
1.B.1c
3.A.1
3.B.1a
3.B.1b
3.C.1a
5.A.1b
5.C.1a
5.C.1b

POSSIBLE TOPICS:

  tigers   tornadoes
  gymnastics   painting
  ant farms   movies about superheroes
  robots as pets   the tallest trees in the world
  amazing buildings

NARROWED TOPIC: _____

TOPIC SENTENCE: _____

_____

Next, make a list of details that support your topic sentence.

DETAILS TO SUPPORT TOPIC SENTENCE: _____

_____

_____

_____

Exercise B Now write a paragraph about the topic you chose for Exercise A. Use the topic sentence and the details you wrote down above. Write a draft of your paragraph on your own paper. Follow the steps for writing a good paragraph that you learned in this chapter. Remember to use the checklists on pages 211 and 213 to check your work before you turn it in to your teacher.

Writing Skills Review

Chapter 11

Excellent Essays

Introduction, Body, and Conclusion

In the previous chapter, you learned how to build a strong paragraph. You begin by writing a topic sentence that tells your main idea. Then you add several sentences that back up, or support, your topic sentence. You use transitions to make the connections between your ideas clear.

In this chapter, you are going to learn how to write several paragraphs that work together to talk about the same topic or general idea. In other words, you will learn how to write an essay. An **essay** is a piece of writing that

- is longer than one paragraph and
- tells about something real (not something imaginary).

A standard essay has three parts:

- The **introduction** is a paragraph that catches the reader's attention. It also tells the main idea, or **thesis,** of the essay. It comes first.

- The **body** is one or more paragraphs long. It presents ideas that support and develop the main idea. It comes after the introduction.

- The **conclusion** is a paragraph that sums up the ideas in the rest of the essay. It comes last, at the end.

228 AIM Higher! ISAT Language Arts Review

Read the following essay a student wrote about his favorite hobby:

Meets ISAT
Standards
1.B.1c
3.B.1a
3.B.1b

One Student's Essay

I live in a house with my mom, my dad, and my little brother. Our house looks like most of the other houses on our street, but it is special. We share it with about forty superheroes and about eighty monsters or bad guys. How could so many superheroes and monsters be living at my house? Well, I did not say that they were living. They are models. Some people call them action figures. For about three years, I have been collecting action figures. Now I can put my own models together. Building your own model action figures can be really interesting and fun.

One reason why building models is so much fun is that you can put different pieces together to make your own heroes or monsters. Some models are made of a few large pieces. I can snap them together quickly. Others, however, are made of a lot of little pieces. These are harder to put together, but the pieces are cool. They make each monster look scary or each superhero look tough. When my dad used to put his own models together, he had to use glue. So, he couldn't take them apart and mix and match the pieces the way I can.

Collecting and building models is also lots of fun because there are so many different kinds available. My models include superheroes, villains, monsters, and soldiers. I also have spaceships and race cars. Some of my models are

More ▶

Introduction, Body, and Conclusion

based on television programs and hit movies. With so many types of models to choose from, it's impossible to get bored collecting them!

Another great reason to build and collect your own models is that you learn to make and paint things yourself. Some models come with the parts already painted. Others have to be painted or decorated with decals that you stick on after assembling the model. I love to make up my own models and to figure out how I want to decorate them. Some of the pieces from different kinds of models do not fit together. But I have lots of choices among the ones that do. If I get stuck when I'm trying to build a model, I can always try what my dad says: If all else fails, try reading the directions.

It's no wonder that building and collecting models has become such a popular hobby. First, it's fun to put your own figures together from all the different pieces. Second, it is fun because of the great variety of models you can get. Third, it is fun because you can build things and then paint or decorate them yourself. If you do not already build and collect models, why not try it? You, too, may find yourself sharing your room with superheroes and monsters!

Planning an Essay

The first step in writing an essay is to plan what you want to say. Choose a topic. Then write a sentence that tells your main idea. This sentence will be your **thesis statement.** After you have written a thesis statement, gather ideas about your topic. Here are some ways you can do this:

Meets ISAT
Standards
1.B.1c
2.B.1a
3.B.1a
3.B.1b
3.C.1a
5.A.1b
5.B.1a
5.C.1a
5.C.1b

- Read about your topic in books and magazines.
- Look up your topic on the Internet. Make sure that the Web pages you use are reliable sources!
- Interview other people about your topic.
- Think about your own past experience. Is it related to your topic in any way?
- Some writers find that it helps to make a list of ideas or create a word web before they begin to write.
- It is a good idea to organize the ideas you have gathered. You can do this by making a rough outline.

Here is a rough outline for the essay on building models:

One Student's Rough Outline

Introduction
—Share house with lots of superheroes & monsters! (say how many)
—Thesis statement (main idea): Building your own model action figures can be really interesting and fun.

More ▶

Introduction, Body, and Conclusion

1st Body Paragraph

Idea for topic sentence: Can put different pieces together to make your own heroes or monsters

—Some have a few large pieces

—Others have lots of little pieces

—Dad used to have to glue pieces together to make his models

—I can snap mine together (easier)

2nd Body Paragraph

Idea for topic sentence: Many types are available

—I have superheroes, villains, monsters, & soldiers

—Also have spaceships & race cars

—Some are based on TV programs & movies

3rd Body Paragraph

Idea for topic sentence: Learn how to make & paint things yourself

—Some already painted—some aren't

—Fun to make your own & figure out how to decorate them— stick on decals

—Some pieces won't fit together, but many do

—If it doesn't work, don't forget to read the directions

Conclusion

Topic sentence: It's no wonder that building and collecting models is so popular.

—Fun to make your own combinations of pieces

—Lots of diff. kinds of models to choose from

—Fun to put them together & decorate them yourself

Your Turn

Exercise A Choose one of the following topics or one of your own and narrow it. Then, write a thesis statement based on your topic. This statement will tell readers what the main idea of your essay will be.

Meets ISAT Standards
3.B.1a
3.B.1b
3.C.1a

TOPICS: your favorite hobby
a movie you really liked
a book you really liked
an interesting place to visit

YOUR NARROWED TOPIC: _____

_____

THESIS STATEMENT: _____

_____

_____

_____

Save this sentence (thesis statement) for another exercise later on.

Your Turn

Exercise B In the space below, make a word web to gather information for your essay. If you need to see what a word web is again, look at page 187.

Exercise C On the lines below, make a rough outline to organize the ideas that you just gathered in your word web. Follow the model on pages 231–32. Save this outline for another exercise later on.

Meets ISAT Standards
3.B.1a
3.B.1b
3.C.1a

Introduction, Body, and Conclusion

Writing the Introduction

The beginning paragraph of an essay is called the **introduction.** In the introduction to an essay, you should

- grab your reader's attention.
- tell readers your thesis, or main idea.

The following chart describes some ways to grab your readers' attention:

Ways to Introduce an Essay
- Begin with a question.
- Begin with a quotation.
- Begin with a very brief story.
- Begin with a surprising or fascinating fact.

236 **AIM Higher! ISAT Language Arts Review**

Here are four different ways you can begin your essay:

Start with a question.

What do you fear most? Some people are afraid of animals like spiders or snakes or bats. Others are afraid of the dark. Still others are afraid of big crowds or of small, cramped spaces. Some people freeze up if they have to talk in front of a large group or audience. However, almost anyone can overcome their fear of public speaking by taking three simple steps.

Start with a quotation.

"Speech is power," wrote Ralph Waldo Emerson. If that is true, then most people are powerless. Many people feel very uncomfortable about speaking in public. In fact, fear of public speaking is one of the most common fears. However, almost anyone can overcome their fear of public speaking by taking three simple steps.

Introduction, Body, and Conclusion

Start with a very brief story.

One time, several years ago, I went to a school talent show. The first performer was supposed to be introduced by a student. The student walked across the stage, stood in front of the microphone, and froze. He stood there for almost a whole minute, saying absolutely nothing. Eventually, a kind teacher came out and led the poor, frightened boy off stage. Not everyone is this afraid of public speaking. This is a common fear, however. Fortunately, almost anyone can overcome their fear of public speaking by taking three simple steps.

Starts with a surprising or fascinating fact.

According to a recent survey, the most common fear of all is fear of public speaking. People fear the unknown. Most people do not have to speak in public every day. As a result, they have little experience with public speaking and are scared by what they do not know. Fortunately, almost anyone can overcome their fear of public speaking by taking three simple steps.

Your Turn

Exercise Write an introduction to your essay on the lines provided below. Make sure that your introduction grabs the attention of your readers. Also make sure that it tells the main idea of your essay. (Use the thesis statement that you wrote for Exercise A on page 233.) You will develop this idea in more detail in the rest of your essay.

Meets ISAT
Standards
3.A.1
3.B.1b
3.C.1a

_____
_____
_____
_____
_____
_____
_____
_____
_____
_____
_____
_____
_____
_____
_____
_____
_____

Introduction, Body, and Conclusion

Writing the Body of the Essay

The **body** is the middle part of an essay. It comes after the introduction. The body of your essay should have at least one paragraph. Some teachers prefer to have their students write at least two or three paragraphs in the body of an essay.

In the body of your essay, you should say more to explain the main idea you brought up in your introduction. Think about the ways you can explain your main idea by bringing in related ideas and details. Each paragraph in the body of your essay should develop an idea that supports, or backs up, your overall idea, or thesis. In the essay on building and collecting models that you read earlier in this chapter, the thesis statement is this:

> Building your own model action figures can be really interesting and fun.

Look, once again, at the rough outline for the body of the essay about building and collecting models:

> 1st Body Paragraph
> Idea for topic sentence: Can put different pieces together to make your own heroes or monsters
> —Some have a few large pieces
> —Others have lots of little pieces
> —Dad used to have to glue pieces together to make his models
> —I can snap mine together (easier)
>
> 2nd Body Paragraph
> Idea for topic sentence: Many types are available
> —I have superheroes, villains, monsters, & soldiers
> —Also have spaceships & race cars
> —Some are based on TV programs & movies
>
> 3rd Body Paragraph
> Idea for topic sentence: Learn how to make & paint things yourself
> —Some already painted—some aren't
> —Fun to make your own & figure out how to decorate them—stick on decals
> —Some pieces won't fit together, but many do
> —If it doesn't work, don't forget to read the directions

Notice how the topic sentence for each body paragraph supports the overall idea of the essay—why collecting and building your own model action figures is fun. Also notice how the details within each paragraph support the topic sentence of that paragraph.

Writing Skills Review 241

Your Turn

Exercise A Go back to the rough outline that you wrote for Exercise C on page 235. Check the middle part of your outline—the part where you show the ideas for your body paragraphs. Write a topic sentence that tells the main idea of each body paragraph. Make sure that each topic sentence supports the overall idea of your whole essay. Also make sure that you have included plenty of details to support each topic sentence. Write your topic sentences on the lines below.

TOPIC SENTENCE OF 1ST BODY PARAGRAPH: _____
_____
_____

TOPIC SENTENCE OF 2ND BODY PARAGRAPH: _____
_____
_____

TOPIC SENTENCE OF 3RD BODY PARAGRAPH: _____
_____
_____

Exercise B On your own paper, write the body paragraphs for your essay. Use the topic sentences that you just created in Exercise A to begin each of your body paragraphs.

Introduction, Body, and Conclusion

Writing the Conclusion

The **conclusion** of an essay is the last part. The conclusion is usually a single paragraph at the end. The conclusion should give your reader a satisfying sense of an ending. Here are some things that you can do to conclude an essay:

- **Summarize,** or put in fewer words, the main ideas that you have given in the rest of the essay.
- Restate your thesis statement (overall idea) in different words.
- Explain the importance of what you have described in the rest of the essay.
- Suggest something that your readers should do.

Of course, you do not have to do all of these things in every conclusion. Take another look at the conclusion to the essay on models. Notice that the writer uses the conclusion to summarize what he said in the rest of the essay. He also calls on the reader to take some action.

> It's no wonder that building and collecting models has become such a popular hobby. First, it's fun to put your own figures together from all the different pieces. Second, it is fun because of the great variety of models you can get. Third, it is fun because you can build things and then paint or decorate them yourself. If you do not already build and collect models, why not try it? You, too, may find yourself sharing your room with superheroes and monsters!

WRITING SKILLS REVIEW **243**

Your Turn

Meets ISAT Standards
3.A.1
3.B.1a
3.B.1b
3.C.1a

Exercise A

- Read the introduction that you wrote for the exercise on page 239.
- Look over your thesis statement and the way you supported your main idea in the body paragraphs you wrote for Exercise B on page 242.
- Now write a rough draft of the conclusion of your essay. Use your own paper.

Exercise B

- Now put together all the pieces of your essay that you have created throughout this chapter—the introduction, body paragraphs, and conclusion.
- Look over your rough draft. Think of ways to make it better. Use the Revision Checklist on page 211 to check your paper.
- Then proofread your revised draft for errors in spelling, grammar, usage, punctuation, and capitalization. Use the checklist on page 213 and the proofreading symbols in the chart on page 214.
- Finally, make a clean copy on your own paper and give it to your teacher.

Return to the questions you answered at the beginning of this unit. Check your work and fix it if necessary. Give your work to your teacher for grading.

Chapter 12
Guided Practice:
Writing about Literature

Step 1 Review pages 154 and 163–64.

Step 2 Read "Time to Stop" on pages 247–49 of this chapter.

Step 3 Choose one of the following topics.

Topic 1: In "Time to Stop," Jimmy discovers a special stopwatch that gives him the power to do something amazing. What does the stopwatch allow him to do? How do you think he is going to use this power? In a paper (essay), describe what Jimmy can do with the stopwatch. Then explain how you think he will use the stopwatch in the future. (Hint: Read the last paragraph in the story one more time.) Use as many details and examples from the story as you can.

Topic 2: "Time to Stop" is fiction, but even a make-believe story should have some parts that could be real. Although many parts of "Time to Stop" could have happened, the story did not really happen. How can you tell for sure that this story is fiction? Which parts of the story are make-believe, and which could have been real? In a paper (essay), explain which parts of the story must be fiction, and which parts seem real. Use as many details and examples from the story as you can.

Meets ISAT Standards
1.B.1c
3.A.1
3.B.1a
3.B.1b
3.C.1a

Guided Practice: Writing about Literature **245**

Guided Practice: Writing about Literature

Step 4 Complete the following story map for "Time to Stop." Part of it has been done for you.

AUTHOR: _____

TITLE: _____

MAIN CHARACTERS: _____

MAIN PROBLEM: *Jimmy has to figure out what the words on the back of his grandfather's watch mean.*

SETTING: _____

MAJOR EVENTS IN PLOT: _____

_____

_____

_____

HOW PROBLEM IS SOLVED: *When Jimmy accidentally freezes his grandmother, he discovers how the watch works. Then he figures out what the words on the back mean. But he still has to learn how to be careful with the watch.*

Step 5 Using the information from your story map, write a rough draft on your own paper. Remember that the introduction should mention the title and author. The introduction should also give the main idea of your paper. Use information from the story to support your answer. Write a conclusion that sums up your ideas.

Step 6 Use the Revision Checklist on page 211 to review your rough draft. Have you done everything the writing prompt asked you to do? Have you used information and examples from the story to support your answer? Is your paper well organized? Create a revised draft.

Step 7 Proofread your revised draft for errors in grammar, usage, capitalization, punctuation, and manuscript form. Refer to the Proofreading Checklist on page 213.

Step 8 Make a clean final copy. Proofread it one last time. Then share it with your classmates and with your teacher.

Meets ISAT Standards
1.B.1b
1.B.1c
2.A.1a
3.A.1
3.B.1a
3.B.1b
3.C.1a

Time to Stop
by Dan Carsen

I had never been up in the attic before. Now that I was old enough, Grandma said, I could look around up there whenever I wanted, as long as she was home. I was excited because I knew there were toys packed in my grandfather's old wooden trunk in the attic. For the first time, I opened the small door and climbed the narrow, rickety steps.

The attic was dark, warm, and musty. It smelled like one big closet, but there was cool stuff everywhere! On a clothes hanger, I saw my grandfather's old Navy uniform. It was almost as white as it looked in the old pictures he used to show me. I saw my grandmother's spelling trophy that she'd won back when she was my age. I even saw a picture of my mother climbing a tree. Everything else might as well have disappeared, though, the moment I saw my grandfather's old trunk.

The big dusty wooden box was painted with faded red letters that said "KEEP OUT!" I was disappointed for a moment until I remembered what Grandma had

More ▶

Guided Practice: Writing about Literature

told me: Before Grandpa died, he had given me special *Top Secret Grandson Permission* to open his trunk, once Grandma said I was old enough. The big day was here.

I ran to the trunk and yanked open the heavy lid. There were so many interesting things inside that I didn't know what to play with first! There were old baseball and football cards. There was a little wooden man attached to two handles that made him dance like crazy when you squeezed them. There was a small bow-and-arrow set, and a soft bulls-eye target to go with it.

I kept digging into the trunk, eager to see everything that was in there. When I got down to the very bottom, I found something strange. It was a stopwatch that looked much newer than anything else in the trunk. Small letters on the back of the stopwatch said, "Be careful about what time you stop." I couldn't figure out what that meant. Even stranger, the stopwatch still seemed to work. It was ticking like a regular watch, but when I pressed its big metal button, a different set of hands started moving and the main hands stopped.

I played with the watch for about twenty minutes. I timed how long I could hold my breath and how long I could balance on one foot. After I got tired, I decided to bring the watch downstairs to ask Grandma about it. As soon as I stepped into the kitchen, she said, "Well *that* was quick. What happened? You get scared up there?"

What did she mean? I had been up there for a long time. I just shook my head and began to ask her about the strange stopwatch. Just as I held it out to her, my thumb brushed against the metal button. My grandmother froze still as a statue. I thought she was playing some kind of game with me, so I said, "C'mon, Grandma. I want to ask you about this."

Normally she would have told me to be more patient and polite, but she didn't move a muscle. She looked just like a perfect statue of herself. She didn't even breathe or blink. The music she had been playing on the radio had suddenly stopped, too. How did she do *that?* I wondered. I started to get a little scared.

"Grandma...Grandma! Stop. That isn't funny." She still didn't move. Grandma had never scared me on purpose before. I began to think something was wrong with her. I ran over to the phone to call my mother at work. When I reached for the

248 AIM Higher! ISAT Language Arts Review

phone, I dropped the watch on the ground. I almost jumped out of my skin when I heard, "J-J-Jimmy? *Jimmy!* How'd you get over there by the phone? I was just looking at you right in front of my face. Boy, you must be really fast."

Things were getting more and more strange each second. I tried to understand what was going on: After I had dropped the watch, my grandmother had started moving again, and the radio had even come back on. I thought about the message on the back of the watch. "Be careful about what time you stop."

Wait...Could it be?

I picked up the watch and pressed the button again. Aha! Just as I thought: Grandma was frozen again, and the radio was silent. I looked up at the big clock on the wall. Its hands weren't moving at all. According to the wall clock, it was 11:45, and the time wasn't changing. I waited for at least two or three minutes, but 11:46 never came. I looked out the window and saw that cars on the street had stopped moving. There was even a beautiful bluebird frozen in midair just outside the window. I walked out the front door and waved at a motionless mailman on the sidewalk.

He didn't move, blink, or seem to notice me at all. It was amazing: The stopwatch from my grandfather's trunk could stop time for everybody and everything except me!

I walked back into the kitchen and over to the phone. I pressed the stopwatch button again. As soon as Grandma came back to life, I said, "Yup. That's right, Grandma. I'm getting *really* fast. Can I go for a walk now?"

As I headed out the door, I noticed my neighbor's small dog sniffing something in the middle of the road. A big truck was speeding toward it. Without even thinking, I pressed the metal button on the stopwatch. Everything froze. I calmly walked out into the street and picked up the little dog. I placed him gently on the sidewalk, then started time again. The truck sped along as if nothing had happened. The dog looked a little confused, but then happily trotted off towards his home.

I began thinking of all the people and animals I could help and all the other fun things I could do. With my grandfather's time-stopping stopwatch, I could be almost like a superhero. Bullies, beware! It was going to be a fun day.

Chapter 13
Guided Practice: Writing Narrative Nonfiction

Step 1: Review the differences between nonfiction and fiction on page 154. Remember that when you are writing a nonfiction narrative, you are telling a story, but it is about real people, places, and events.

Step 2: Choose one of the following topics or one of your own. If you choose your own topic, make sure that it is autobiographical (about yourself) or biographical (about someone else). Remember to show your topic to your teacher before you begin writing.

Topic 1: Think of a time when you did something that made you feel very proud. Perhaps you did something kind for another person or for an animal. Perhaps you won an award or did something you had thought you would not be able to do. In a paper (essay), tell what you did and why. Explain why you felt proud. Use specific details to make the story interesting.

Topic 2: Sometimes people learn by having bad experiences. Making mistakes is one way that people learn important lessons. Write a paper (essay) about a time when you or someone else learned from making a mistake. What happened? What lesson was learned? If you choose to write about someone else, the person can be living or dead. You may need to do some research at the library or on the Internet. In your paper, be sure to give examples of how the person learned from his or her mistake.

If you choose a topic of your own, describe that topic here:

_____

250 AIM Higher! ISAT Language Arts Review

Step 3 List the main conflict, or problem, that will be presented in your paper. If you choose a topic of your own that does not involve a conflict, write "no conflict" here.

_____

Meets ISAT Standards
1.B.1b
1.B.1c
3.B.1a
3.B.1b
3.C.1a
5.A.1b
5.B.1a
5.C.1b

Step 4 On your own paper, make a timeline or a list of the people, places, and events that you will include in your writing.

Step 5 Complete the following sensory detail chart. List specific details that you will use to make your essay realistic and interesting.

Sight	Sound	Touch	Taste	Smell

Guided Practice: Writing Narrative Nonfiction

Guided Practice:
Narrative Nonfiction

Step 6 Explain why the subject of your paper is important. Tell what lesson a reader might learn from your paper. You will use this information in the conclusion of your essay.

_____

_____

_____

_____

_____

Step 7 Using the information that you have gathered, write a rough draft on your own paper.

Step 8 Use the Revision Checklist on page 211 to review your rough draft. Have you presented your events in time order? Have you used enough details to make the people, places, and events come alive in your readers' minds? Have you included information about who the characters are and what they are like? Have you written a conclusion that tells why what happens in your paper is important? Create a revised draft.

Step 9 Proofread your revised draft for errors in grammar, usage, capitalization, punctuation, and manuscript form. Refer to the Proofreading Checklist on page 213.

Step 10 Make a clean final copy. Proofread it one last time. Then share it with your classmates and with your teacher.

Chapter 14

Guided Practice: Writing Expository, or Informative, Nonfiction

Step 1 Review pages 154–56.

Step 2 Choose one of the following topics or one of your own. If you choose your own topic, make sure that the topic is for a piece of writing that informs, or tells facts. Remember to show your topic to your teacher before you begin writing.

Meets ISAT Standards
1.B.1b
1.B.1c
3.A.1
3.B.1a
3.B.1b
3.C.1a
5.A.1b
5.B.1a
5.C.1b

Topic 1: Many different kinds of living things help people. Plants make food, medicine, wood, and what we need to breathe. Some other examples of living things that help humans are pets, horses, and honeybees. Choose one kind of creature (plant or animal) that helps people. Write a paper (essay) explaining how that type of creature helps us. You will probably have to do some research at the library or on the Internet.

Topic 2: Choose something that you have learned about in school. It could be a sport or a game. It could be a historical event or a way to solve math problems. It could be a new way to write or draw. It could be something you learned in science class. Write a paper (essay) that describes what you have learned in detail.

If you choose a topic of your own, describe that topic here:

_____

_____

Step 3 On your own paper, create a word web to gather information about your topic.

Guided Practice: Expository, or Informative, Nonfiction

Step 4 On the lines below and on the next page, create a rough outline for your informative essay.

INTRODUCTION

LEAD (SOMETHING TO GRAB THE READER'S ATTENTION): _____
_____

THESIS STATEMENT: _____
_____

FIRST BODY PARAGRAPH

    MAIN IDEA: _____
    _____

    SUPPORTING DETAILS: _____
    _____
    _____

SECOND BODY PARAGRAPH

    MAIN IDEA: _____
    _____

    SUPPORTING DETAILS: _____
    _____
    _____

THIRD BODY PARAGRAPH

    MAIN IDEA: _____
    _____

More ▶

SUPPORTING DETAILS: _____

_____

_____

CONCLUSION: _____

_____

Meets ISAT Standards
1.B.1b
1.B.1c
3.A.1
3.B.1a
3.B.1b
3.C.1a
5.A.1b
5.B.1a
5.C.1b

Step 5 Using your graphic organizer and rough outline, write a rough draft on your own paper. Make sure to include an introduction with a thesis statement. The thesis statement should tell your main idea. You will expand and support this main idea in the body of your essay. The body should have at least two or three paragraphs. Remember to write a conclusion that brings your paper to a satisfying close. Present facts, not opinions. Present your ideas in an order that makes sense.

Step 6 Use the Revision Checklist on page 211 to review your rough draft. Have you presented only facts, not opinions? Have you presented enough information (specific details and examples) to support your thesis statement? Are your ideas clear? Are they presented in an order that makes sense? Revise your draft.

Step 7 Proofread your revised draft for errors in grammar, usage, capitalization, punctuation, and manuscript form. Refer to the Proofreading Checklist on page 213.

Step 8 Make a clean final copy. Proofread it one last time. Then share it with your classmates and with your teacher.

Chapter 15
Guided Practice:
Writing Persuasive Nonfiction

Step 1 Review pages 154–56.

Step 2 Choose one of the following topics or one of your own. If you choose your own topic, make sure that the topic is for a persuasive essay. Remember to show your topic to your teacher before you begin writing.

Topic 1: The average child in America watches three to four hours of television each day. Do you think that this is good or bad? Do children learn good lessons from television, or do children see all sorts of bad things on television? Does watching television keep children out of trouble, or does it keep them from doing more important activities? Write a paper (essay) explaining your opinion. Support your opinion with as many facts as possible. You may use your own experiences or information you gather in the library or on the Internet.

Topic 2: Your class is having a "Teacher for a Day" contest. Write a letter to your principal explaining why you would be the best student teacher for your class. Would you be able to plan a good lesson? Could you explain the lesson to the class? Could you help students with their work? How would you handle students who don't pay attention or act up? Try to persuade your principal that *you* should be "Teacher for a Day."

If you choose a topic of your own, describe that topic here:

_____
_____

Step 3 On your own paper, create a word web or chart to help gather and organize ideas for your topic.

Step 4 In the space below and on the next page, create a rough outline for your paper (persuasive essay). Think about the order in which you will make your arguments. Will you present the strongest reason first or last?

Meets ISAT Standards
1.B.1b
1.B.1c
3.B.1a
3.B.1b
3.C.1a
5.A.1b
5.B.1a
5.C.1b

INTRODUCTION

LEAD (SOMETHING TO GRAB THE READER'S ATTENTION): _____

_____

THESIS STATEMENT: _____

_____

FIRST BODY PARAGRAPH

    MAIN IDEA: _____

_____

    SUPPORTING DETAILS: _____

_____

_____

SECOND BODY PARAGRAPH

    MAIN IDEA: _____

_____

    SUPPORTING DETAILS: _____

_____

More ▶

Guided Practice: Writing Persuasive Nonfiction

Guided Practice: Persuasive Nonfiction

Meets ISAT
Standards
3.A.1
3.B.1a
3.B.1b
3.C.1a

THIRD BODY PARAGRAPH

MAIN IDEA: _____
_____

SUPPORTING DETAILS: _____
_____
_____

CONCLUSION: _____
_____

Step 5 Using the information that you have gathered above, write a rough draft on your own paper.

Step 6 Use the Revision Checklist on page 211 to review your rough draft. Does it have a well-developed beginning, middle, and end? Have you presented a clear opinion in your thesis statement? Have you supported your opinion with facts? Did you present your facts and reasons in an order that makes sense? Is your paper convincing? Create a revised draft.

Step 7 Proofread your revised draft for errors in grammar, usage, capitalization, punctuation, and manuscript form. Refer to the Proofreading Checklist on page 213.

Step 8 Make a clean final copy. Proofread it one last time. Then share it with your classmates and with your teacher.

AIM Higher! ISAT Language Arts Review

Posttest

ISAT for Reading
ISAT for Writing

Posttest

ISAT for Reading and Writing

This Posttest is like the Illinois Standards Achievement Test (ISAT) for Reading and the Illinois Standards Achievement Test (ISAT) for Writing. The Posttest is organized as follows:

Part 1: ISAT for Reading

Session 1: Fourteen word-analysis questions and one reading selection with multiple-choice questions

Session 2: One reading selection with multiple-choice questions and an extended-response question

Session 3: One reading selection with multiple-choice questions and an extended-response question

Part 2: ISAT for Writing

Response to one writing prompt chosen by the student

ISAT for Reading: SESSION 1

Word Analysis

Directions Your teacher will read each question. Fill in the bubble of the letter next to the correct answer. All of these questions have only one correct answer. Do not begin until your teacher gives you directions.

1. *The garden walkway was made of old, red* **bricks.**

   Which word <u>begins</u> with the same sounds as **bricks**?
   - Ⓐ borrow
   - Ⓑ better
   - Ⓒ bridle
   - Ⓓ blend

2. *A fly landed on the* **ceiling.**

   Which word <u>begins</u> with the same sound as **ceiling**?
   - Ⓐ careful
   - Ⓑ softly
   - Ⓒ content
   - Ⓓ sharp

3. What does **inactive** mean?
   - Ⓐ very active
   - Ⓑ too active
   - Ⓒ slightly active
   - Ⓓ not active

4. How many syllables does the word **tornado** have?
   - Ⓐ one syllable
   - Ⓑ two syllables
   - Ⓒ three syllables
   - Ⓓ four syllables

Posttest

5. Which word has the same sound as the letters "ir" in **shirt**?
   - Ⓐ court
   - Ⓑ short
   - Ⓒ curb
   - Ⓓ smart

6. What does the word **hopeless** mean?
   - Ⓐ without hope
   - Ⓑ full of hope
   - Ⓒ feeling hope
   - Ⓓ one who hopes

7. Which word has the same sound as the letters "oo" in **book**?
   - Ⓐ tooth
   - Ⓑ cook
   - Ⓒ door
   - Ⓓ moose

8. *The students were glad to read a new book.*

   Which word begins with the same sounds as **glad**?
   - Ⓐ glide
   - Ⓑ grind
   - Ⓒ girl
   - Ⓓ gallop

9. In which word do the letters "ch" sound the same as the letters "ck" in **back**?
   - Ⓐ rich
   - Ⓑ which
   - Ⓒ ache
   - Ⓓ pitch

**PART 1: ISAT for Reading
SESSION 1**

10. Which word is made from the words **ground** and **play**?

    Ⓐ playgroup

    Ⓑ playground

    Ⓒ groundhog

    Ⓓ playroom

11. What is the root of **suitable**?

    Ⓐ table

    Ⓑ tab

    Ⓒ able

    Ⓓ suit

12. *I had a **fun** day at the county fair.*

    What word has the same "u" sound as the letter "u" in **fun**?

    Ⓐ fur

    Ⓑ due

    Ⓒ full

    Ⓓ tunnel

13. What word has the same "i" sound as the letter "i" in **promise**?

    Ⓐ exercise

    Ⓑ thigh

    Ⓒ mitt

    Ⓓ wise

14. Which word <u>ends</u> with the same sound that begins the word **fun**?

    Ⓐ tooth

    Ⓑ flight

    Ⓒ sift

    Ⓓ enough

GO ON

Posttest

ISAT for Reading: SESSION 1, continued

Directions This selection is about a boy who is nervous about going on a class field trip. Read the selection. Then answer multiple-choice questions 15 through 28.

Class Trip
by Francis McQuade

Ms. Andrew's class was going on their first class trip. They were going to the firehouse. Everyone was very excited, except for Terry, that is. All the other kids were talking about the trip they would take the next day, but Terry sat quietly at his desk.

"What's wrong, Terry?" his friend Ellen asked.

"I'm not sure I'm coming to school tomorrow."

"Why?" Ellen asked. "You'll miss the field trip."

"I don't want to go to the fire station," Terry said softly.

"Why not?" Ellen asked.

"What if there's a fire when we're there? Will the firefighters and the trucks have to rush out? What will happen to us?" he asked. Terry was nervous about going on the field trip. He really wanted to see the big red fire trucks, but he didn't like going to new places. He worried about whether he would be able to get around easily in his wheelchair.

"Don't worry," said Ellen. "Even if that happens, I'm sure we'll be safe. They have a plan for something like that." Ellen knew a lot about firefighters. Terry had never been to a firehouse, but Ellen had. Her uncle was a firefighter. Ellen had a picture in her room of her Uncle Fred next to a big fire truck.

Terry felt a little less nervous, but he still looked unsure about going.

264 AIM Higher! ISAT LANGUAGE ARTS REVIEW

"The firefighters are there to protect us, Terry." Ellen said. "They wouldn't let anything bad happen to us. Besides, it won't be any fun without you," she added. At that, Terry smiled a little.

The next morning, Ellen was happy to see Terry waiting outside the school with the rest of the class. She gave his shoulder a squeeze. "This is going to be great," she said with a wink.

When the school bus got to the firehouse, Terry waited until the other kids got off. Then his helper carried him off, put him in his wheelchair, and pushed him inside. Terry's jaw dropped when he saw the trucks up close. They were huge and bright red and really shiny. He rolled his wheelchair over to one. The tires were taller than his chair.

A group of kids were with a firefighter named Sarah. She showed them the heavy coats and hats the firefighters wear. She even let them try on the big boots the firefighters wear to keep their feet dry.

Another group of kids stood beside one of the trucks. A firefighter named Steve was pointing out the controls inside the truck. Terry tried to push himself up higher to see. It was no use.

Steve noticed Terry struggling to see and said, "Do you want to sit inside the truck?" Terry nodded. "First you need a hat," said Steve. He took one of the firefighters' hats off a hook and put it on Terry's head. "Now you look like a firefighter," he said. He picked Terry up and gently slid him into the cab of the fire truck. Then he pointed out some of the buttons and switches.

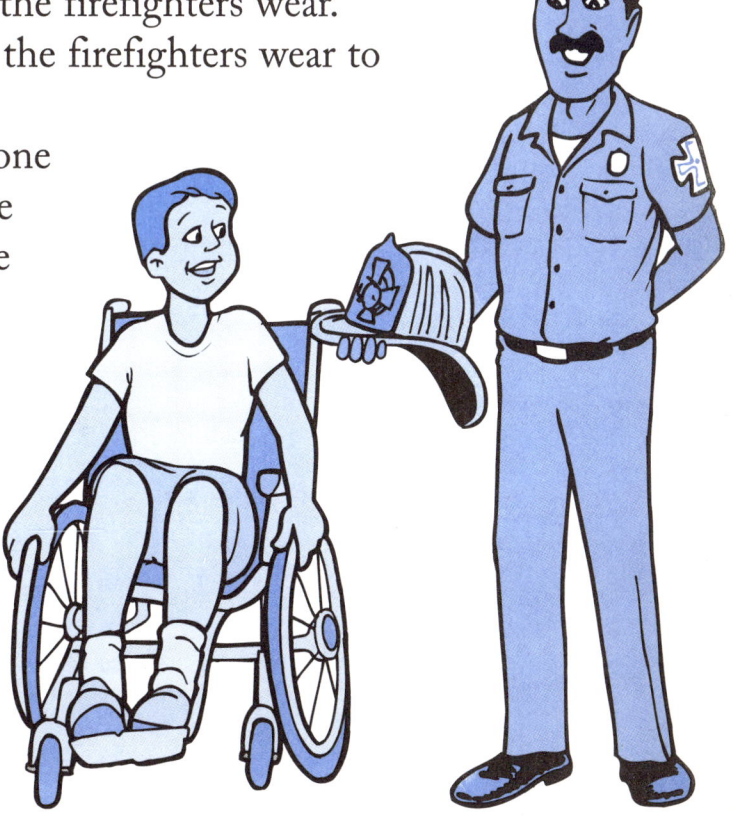

Posttest

"There's the radio. You press here to talk," said Steve. "Are you ready for something fun? Push this button." Terry pushed it and the lights on the truck started to flash. "There's the siren. Do you want to hear it?" Steve asked. Terry's eyes lit up. Did he ever! He whispered in Steve's ear.

"Where's Ellen?" the fireman called. Ellen walked shyly over to the truck. "Terry here says you might like to try the siren," Steve said. Ellen nodded eagerly. She climbed into the cab next to Terry and pushed a button. The huge whoop of the siren filled the station house.

The fireman reached in and turned it off. "OK. That's enough," he said with a grin.

The whole class came over to the truck. "Wow!" they said when they saw Terry and Ellen inside. "Where did you get that hat? Did you really get to turn on the siren? Lucky!"

Steve helped Terry back into his chair. Ellen leaned over and spoke quietly to Terry. "See. There was nothing to worry about. This place is pretty neat, huh?"

"It sure is," answered Terry, "I wonder where we'll go on the next field trip."

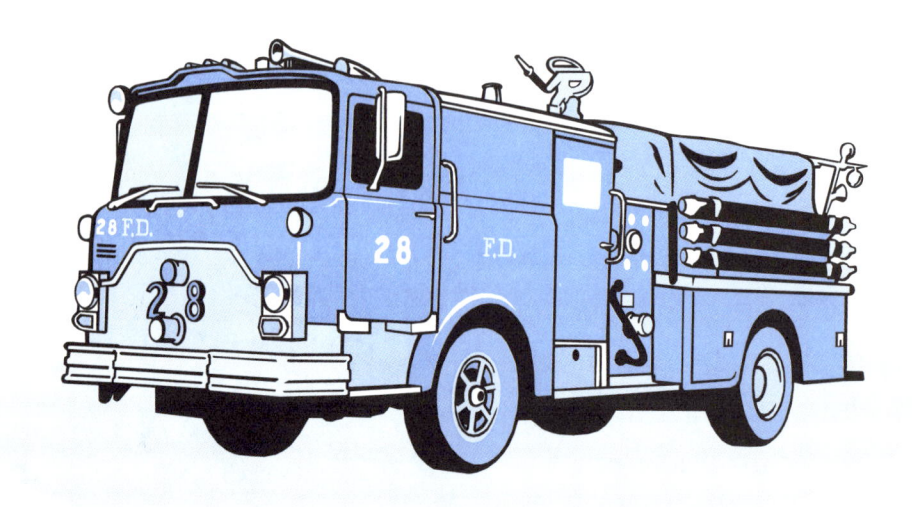

PART 1: ISAT for Reading
SESSION 1

Directions For each question, choose the best answer. You may look back at the selection at any time.

"Class Trip," by Francis McQuade

15. What is this story mostly about?
    - Ⓐ how to become a firefighter
    - Ⓑ why everyone should have a hero
    - Ⓒ a boy who is afraid of new places
    - Ⓓ a girl who is afraid of fire trucks

16. Which word best describes Terry at the beginning of the story?
    - Ⓐ worried
    - Ⓑ excited
    - Ⓒ happy
    - Ⓓ angry

17. Why do their classmates say that Terry and Ellen are lucky?
    - Ⓐ because they get to slide down the firefighters' pole
    - Ⓑ because they get to wear a firefighter's hat and sound the siren
    - Ⓒ because they get to try on a firefighter's boots and coat
    - Ⓓ because they get to meet Terry's Uncle Steve

18. By the end of the story, how has Terry changed?
    - Ⓐ He wants to save other people.
    - Ⓑ He is no longer friends with Ellen.
    - Ⓒ He is not nervous about field trips.
    - Ⓓ He has made new friends in school.

GO ON

Posttest

19. What does the first illustration in the story show?
    - Ⓐ that Terry wants to be a firefighter
    - Ⓑ that Terry is still nervous about the trip
    - Ⓒ that Terry wants to go back to school
    - Ⓓ that Terry is having fun on the field trip

20. If Terry had to write about his class trip, who would he probably mention in his writing?
    - Ⓐ Steve and Ellen
    - Ⓑ his mother and Ellen
    - Ⓒ his uncle and Steve
    - Ⓓ his teacher and Ellen

21. Why is Terry worried about going to the firehouse?
    - Ⓐ He is nervous about visiting a new place in his wheelchair.
    - Ⓑ He is scared of loud sounds, so he is worried that they will sound the siren.
    - Ⓒ He does not want to go without his friend Ellen, and she is home sick.
    - Ⓓ He is worried that he will not make it back to school in time for lunch.

22. How does Ellen make Terry feel better about the field trip?
    - Ⓐ She lets him sit next to her on the bus.
    - Ⓑ She promises him that he can sit in a fire truck.
    - Ⓒ She tells him that the firefighters will keep them safe.
    - Ⓓ She makes him talk to her uncle about firehouses.

PART 1: ISAT for Reading
SESSION 1

23. How does Terry get on and off the bus?
    Ⓐ He rolls his wheelchair up and down the steps.
    Ⓑ A machine lifts him up and down.
    Ⓒ His helper carries him.
    Ⓓ Ellen carries him.

24. Terry's jaw drops when he sees the fire trucks up close. What does the author mean when she says that "his jaw drops"?
    Ⓐ He is fearful.
    Ⓑ He is amazed.
    Ⓒ He is bored.
    Ⓓ He is lazy.

25. Which of the following events happens last?
    Ⓐ Terry flashes the lights of the fire truck.
    Ⓑ Ellen pushes the button for the fire siren.
    Ⓒ Steve puts Terry into the fire truck.
    Ⓓ Sarah lets the children try on firefighters' boots.

26. Terry struggles to see inside the fire truck. What does it mean to *struggle*?
    Ⓐ to work hard
    Ⓑ to give up
    Ⓒ to push others
    Ⓓ to sit down

Posttest

27. Why does the author have Terry say, "I wonder where we'll go on the next field trip"?

- Ⓐ to show that he is ready to go back to the school
- Ⓑ to show that he listened to his friend Ellen
- Ⓒ to show that he really likes to be out of school
- Ⓓ to show that he is no longer worried about new places

28. What is one theme of this story?

- Ⓐ Everyone has the same skills and talents.
- Ⓑ Anyone can become a firefighter.
- Ⓒ Overcoming fear can bring great rewards.
- Ⓓ Some jobs are more fun than others.

End of PART 1: SESSION 1

PART 1: ISAT for Reading
SESSION 2

ISAT for Reading: SESSION 2

Directions This story is an African myth about how Anansi the spider brought stories to the people. Read the story. Then answer multiple-choice questions 29 through 48 and the extended-response question.

How Anansi the Spider Brought Stories to the People
A myth retold by Marco Campos

A long time ago, the people of West Africa did not have any stories. All the world's stories belonged to the Sky God. He kept them all locked away in a golden box.

Fortunately for the people, Anansi the Spider was a great hero. And what made him a hero was his intelligence. He was the craftiest of all the creatures. Anansi loved stories. He wanted the Sky God's stories so he could tell them to the people. So, Anansi spun a thread and climbed up to the heavens. There he found the Sky God, admiring his golden box.

"Sky God," said Anansi. "You have so many stories. Wouldn't you like to share some of them with the people?"

"Not really," said the Sky God. "My stories are worth a lot. I will let you have them only if you do a few things for me."

"What would you like for me to do?" asked Anansi.

"A few simple things," said the Sky God. "First, I would like you to bring me the bees that swarm and sting. Then, I want you to bring me the giant python that swallows men whole. Next, bring me the leopard with teeth as sharp as spears. Finally, bring me the Queen of the Fairies, who is never seen. If you do all these things for me, then I shall give you my golden box of stories."

GO ON

Posttest

Anansi climbed back down his thread, thinking all the while. Back on solid ground, he found an empty gourd and filled it with water. Then he walked through the forest until he found a beehive hanging from a tree limb. He climbed the tree and sprinkled water into the hive. He poured the rest of the water on himself and covered his head with a banana leaf. When he had done all this, he called out to the bees, "The rain has come, foolish bees. Quick, fly into the gourd and protect yourselves. Otherwise, you might drown."

Startled, the bees flew into the gourd, thanking Anansi all the while. When they were inside, Anansi spun a web around the opening in the gourd so they couldn't get out. He took the gourd full of bees to the Sky God. The Sky God was amazed but said, "You still have three more tasks to do."

Anansi returned to the forest and found a tall bamboo plant. He cut a pole from this plant and lifted it onto his shoulder. Then he walked to the house of the giant python. As he walked, he talked to himself. "This pole is longer than the snake. You are wrong. Python is much longer. Is not. Is too."

Python was listening. "Why are you talking to yourself, Anansi?" said Python.

"No. I was talking to my wife," said Anansi. She thinks that you are shorter than this pole, but I said that you were much longer."

"There's an easy way to solve that argument," said Python. "I shall lie down next to the pole. Then you will see how long and mighty I am."

Now Anansi knew that Python and the bamboo pole were the same length.

Python stretched out next to the pole. "Foolish snake," cried Anansi as he spun threads to bind Python to the pole. Try as he would, Python could not struggle free. Anansi carried the pole, with Python tied to it, to the Sky God. Sky God said, "But you still have two more tasks."

Anansi returned to the forest. He dug a deep pit and covered it with leaves. Leopard fell in. Anansi sprinkled dust on Leopard that made him go to sleep. Then he brought Leopard to the Sky God.

"You have one more task," said the Sky God. "But it is the hardest of all." The Sky God believed that there was no way that Anansi could catch the Queen of the Fairies, for she was invisible.

Anansi carved a doll out of wood and covered it with sticky tree sap. Anansi knew that fairies love to steal dolls. Anansi left the doll under an odum tree, where fairies like to play. After a while, the Fairy Queen came through the woods. The Fairy Queen saw the doll and grabbed it. The doll stuck tight to her hand. She could not shake it off. She started to run away, but Anansi followed the doll. Eventually, he caught the Fairy Queen. He spun a web around her and carried her to the Sky God.

"You have done great things," said the Sky God. "Because of your intelligence, you have done what strong warriors could not do."

So, Sky God gave Anansi his golden box full of stories. When Anansi opened the box, the stories all flew out and into Anansi's ear. Thereafter, Anansi told the stories day and night. That's how there came to be so many stories in the world. This story has been one of them.

Posttest

Directions For each question, choose the best answer. You may look back at the selection as often as necessary.

"How Anansi the Spider Brought Stories to the People," A myth retold by Marco Campos

29. Where does most of the action of the story take place?
    - Ⓐ in the sky
    - Ⓑ in the forest
    - Ⓒ in a snake pit
    - Ⓓ in a spider's web

30. What wonderful thing does Anansi get for the people of Earth?
    - Ⓐ music
    - Ⓑ food
    - Ⓒ dance
    - Ⓓ stories

31. The Sky God gives Anansi some tasks. What is a *task*?
    - Ⓐ a gift
    - Ⓑ a story
    - Ⓒ something to do
    - Ⓓ something to wear

32. Which of the following words best describes the Sky God?
    - Ⓐ stingy
    - Ⓑ generous
    - Ⓒ kind
    - Ⓓ cruel

**PART 1: ISAT for Reading
SESSION 2**

33. How does the Sky God respond to Anansi when he brings him the bees, the python, and the leopard?
    Ⓐ He gets mad and sends Anansi away.
    Ⓑ He stomps around and throws lightning bolts.
    Ⓒ He claps and laughs with glee.
    Ⓓ He reminds Anansi that he has more tasks to do.

34. Which of the following could be another title for this story?
    Ⓐ "Why Spiders Spin Webs"
    Ⓑ "Animals of Africa"
    Ⓒ "Where Stories Come From"
    Ⓓ "Stay Away from Fairies"

35. Why did Anansi cover his head with a banana leaf?
    Ⓐ to hide from the stinging bees
    Ⓑ to look like he was hiding from the rain
    Ⓒ to drip water on the bees
    Ⓓ to gather sleeping dust to capture the leopard

36. Why do the bees fly into the gourd?
    Ⓐ to escape from the python
    Ⓑ to escape drowning in the rain
    Ⓒ to escape the Sky God
    Ⓓ to escape from the leopard

37. A gourd is most like which of the following objects?
    Ⓐ a stick
    Ⓑ a box
    Ⓒ a plate
    Ⓓ a pitcher

GO ON

Posttest

38. The giant python is measured against which of these?
- Ⓐ an odum tree
- Ⓑ a spider's thread
- Ⓒ a bamboo pole
- Ⓓ a tall termite mound

39. Why does Anansi argue with himself?
- Ⓐ to fool Python into thinking that he is arguing with his wife
- Ⓑ to fool Python into thinking that there are hunters in the forest
- Ⓒ to fool Leopard into joining the argument
- Ⓓ to fool Leopard into thinking that there are hunters in the forest

40. How is Anansi able to bring Leopard to the Sky God without getting bitten?
- Ⓐ He sings to Leopard to keep him calm and happy.
- Ⓑ He makes a deal with Leopard to free him if he does not bite Anansi.
- Ⓒ He sprinkles dust on Leopard to put him to sleep.
- Ⓓ He ties Leopard's mouth with thread so that he cannot bite.

41. How does Anansi catch the Fairy Queen?
- Ⓐ He blows magic powder on her.
- Ⓑ He watches for her footprints in the mud.
- Ⓒ He waits for the moon to come out.
- Ⓓ He follows a doll that is stuck to her hand.

**PART 1: ISAT for Reading
SESSION 2**

42. Why does the Sky God think that there is no way that Anansi will be able to catch the Fairy Queen?
    - Ⓐ because she is too smart
    - Ⓑ because she is too fast
    - Ⓒ because she is invisible
    - Ⓓ because she is not real

43. How is Anansi able to catch the bees, Python, Leopard and Fairy Queen?
    - Ⓐ Anansi entertains them with stories so that they will follow him.
    - Ⓑ Anansi is able to trap the animals because he knows the way they act.
    - Ⓒ Anansi makes the animals angry so they fall into his traps.
    - Ⓓ Anansi sprinkles a magic powder on them to make them fall asleep.

44. Anansi tells the bees and the python that they are foolish. What does the word *foolish* mean?
    - Ⓐ brave and heroic
    - Ⓑ clever and tricky
    - Ⓒ mighty and powerful
    - Ⓓ silly and stupid

45. For which activity in the story did Anansi most need his thread?
    - Ⓐ to climb up to the heavens
    - Ⓑ to dig a deep pit
    - Ⓒ to cut down the bamboo plant
    - Ⓓ to hollow out the gourd

Posttest

46. Where does Anansi get the tools that he needs to complete his tasks?

    Ⓐ He borrows the tools from the Sky God.
    Ⓑ He steals the tools from the village.
    Ⓒ He finds the tools in the forest.
    Ⓓ He buys the tools from the people.

47. What happened after the Sky God gave Anansi his box full of stories?

    Ⓐ Anansi dropped the box and lost all the stories.
    Ⓑ Anansi spread the stories among the people on Earth.
    Ⓒ Anansi took the box and gave the stories back to the Sky God.
    Ⓓ Anansi opened the box, and the stories flew into his ear.

48. What quality helps Anansi to succeed?

    Ⓐ his great strength
    Ⓑ his knowledge of weapons
    Ⓒ his knowledge of battle plans and tactics
    Ⓓ his intelligence

**PART 1: ISAT for Reading
SESSION 2**

Extended-Response Question

49. In the story, Anansi is described as the "craftiest of all creatures." Think about what the word *crafty* means. Use examples and details from the story to explain how Anansi is crafty.

_____

_____

_____

_____

_____

_____

_____

_____

_____

_____

_____

_____

End of PART 1: SESSION 2   STOP

Note to Students: Your written response will be scored using a rubric like the one on page 54.

Posttest

ISAT for Reading: SESSION 3

Directions This selection tells about a famous ship that was lost for more than three hundred years. Read the selection. Then answer multiple-choice questions 50 through 69 and the extended-response question.

The *Vasa*
by Robert Kaufman

Sweden is a country in northern Europe. In the early 1600s, Sweden was trying to build an empire around the Baltic Sea. The people of Sweden were proud of their strong navy. Their king decided to build the biggest warship in the world. The ship was to be called the *Vasa*.

On Sunday, August 10, 1628, the *Vasa* was ready to take its first trip. People stood along the beaches of Stockholm, Sweden's capital city. They were there to watch the ship leave the harbor.

Just minutes after setting sail, the *Vasa* began to tip over. The people along the shore watched in horror. For a moment, the ship seemed to stand back up. But then it fell over again! Water began to rush in through the open gun ports. Soon the ship sank.

Why did the *Vasa* sink? No one knows for sure. A ship so large had never been built before. Some people think that the builders did not really know how to build such a big ship. Other people think that the boat was too heavy on top. It had two rows of decks above the waterline. Each deck was loaded with heavy guns. There were sixty-four guns in all. Ships built before that time had only one row of guns. A few people think that the ship was too narrow and too tall. If the boat had been wider, they say, it might not have tipped over so easily. Finally, some people blame the ship's captain for sinking the ship because he left the gun ports open.

The *Vasa* lay at the bottom of the harbor for more than three hundred years. Then, in 1956, after several years of searching, a shipwreck expert found the *Vasa*. He wanted to raise the *Vasa* out of the water. He had no trouble

Posttest

gaining support for his plan, but raising the ship was not so easy! It took another five years to bring the ship up from the bottom of the harbor.

On April 24, 1961, the *Vasa* was finally raised to the surface of the water. The entire country of Sweden seemed to come to a halt on that day. Most Swedes stopped what they were doing to watch the event on television. After 333 years under water, the *Vasa* had been recovered.

Parts of the ship had to be rebuilt. Yet the *Vasa* was in very good shape for such an old ship. Today, it is kept inside a museum. The Vasa Museum is the most popular museum in Sweden. About eight hundred thousand people from Sweden and all around the world visit the museum each year.

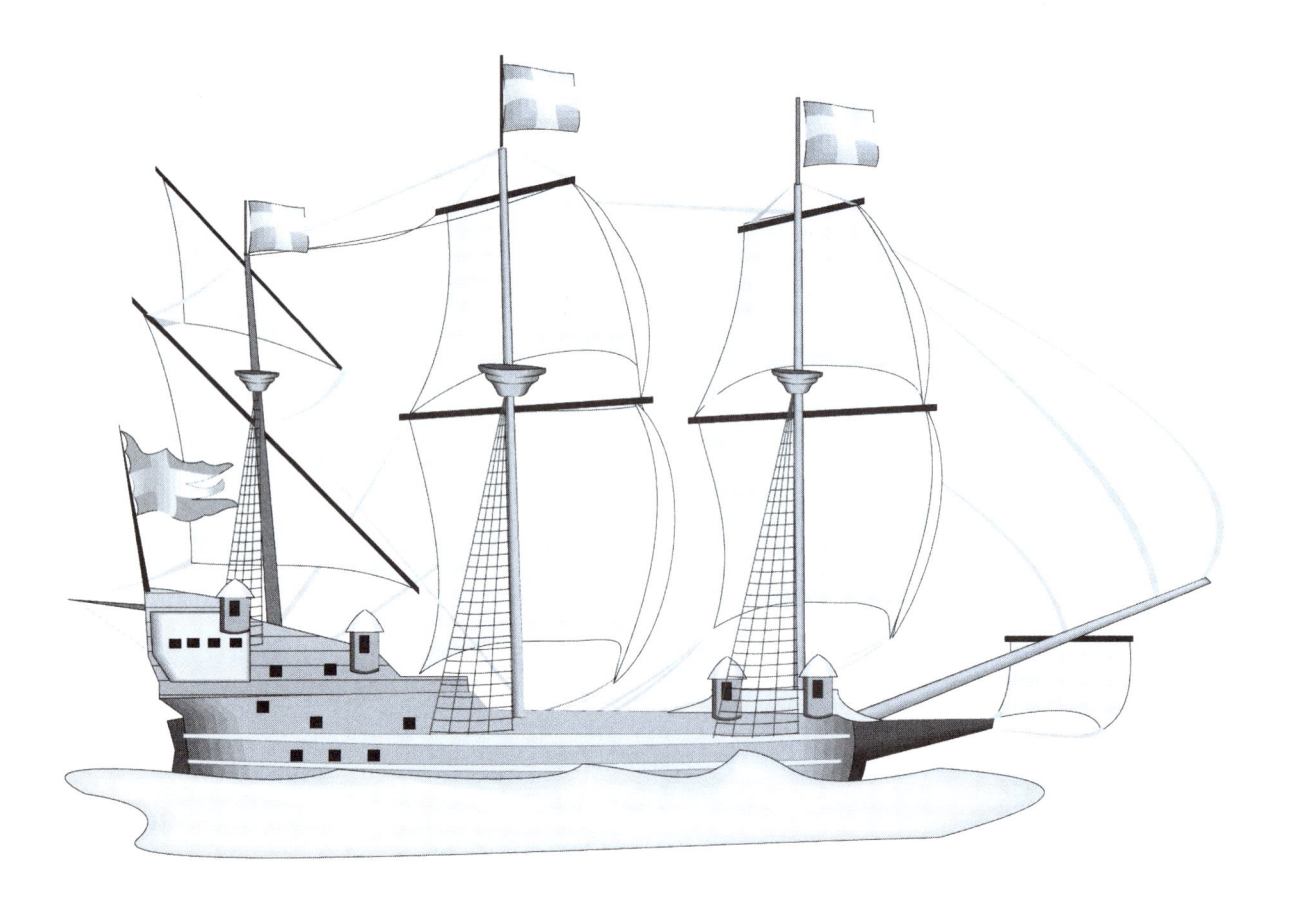

PART 1: ISAT for Reading
SESSION 3

Directions For each question, choose the best answer. You may look back at the selection as often as necessary.

"The *Vasa*," by Robert Kaufman

50. What is the *Vasa*?
    - Ⓐ a country in northern Europe
    - Ⓑ a Swedish warship
    - Ⓒ the Swedish word for "navy"
    - Ⓓ the name of the king of Sweden

51. After being missing for many years, the *Vasa* was recovered. Which of the following items can be *recovered*?
    - Ⓐ a rotten egg
    - Ⓑ a broken window
    - Ⓒ a lost wallet
    - Ⓓ an open door

52. Why did the king of Sweden want to build the *Vasa*?
    - Ⓐ He wanted to watch the ship sink into the Baltic Sea.
    - Ⓑ He was trying to learn how to sail on the ship.
    - Ⓒ He wanted to give it as a gift to the queen.
    - Ⓓ He was trying to build an empire around the Baltic Sea.

53. What might be one reason that the *Vasa* sank?
    - Ⓐ It was carrying too many people.
    - Ⓑ It was attacked by the enemy.
    - Ⓒ The captain left the gun ports open.
    - Ⓓ It was an old, broken-down ship.

GO ON

Posttest

54. How was the *Vasa* different from other ships that were built before it?
- Ⓐ It had two decks for guns.
- Ⓑ People were proud of it.
- Ⓒ It was wide and tall.
- Ⓓ It was built for the Swedish navy.

55. For how long did the *Vasa* lie under water?
- Ⓐ 56 years
- Ⓑ 200 years
- Ⓒ 333 years
- Ⓓ 107 years

56. People stood along the beaches of Stockholm to watch the ship leave the harbor. What happened first as the ship set sail?
- Ⓐ the ship tipped over
- Ⓑ the ship sank
- Ⓒ water rushed through the open gun ports
- Ⓓ the ship's guns were fired

57. The people on the beaches watched in horror as the ship began to tip over. What is *horror*?
- Ⓐ shock and fear
- Ⓑ calmness
- Ⓒ pride
- Ⓓ excitement

PART 1: ISAT for Reading
SESSION 3

58. How many guns did the *Vasa* have?
- Ⓐ 4
- Ⓑ 64
- Ⓒ 300
- Ⓓ 1,956

59. Which of these events did not happen?
- Ⓐ The captain of the *Vasa* closed the gun ports before setting sail.
- Ⓑ A shipwreck expert found the *Vasa* at the bottom of the harbor.
- Ⓒ The *Vasa* sank soon after it set sail.
- Ⓓ Many Swedes watched the raising of the *Vasa* on television.

60. What probably happened as a result of the sinking of the *Vasa*?
- Ⓐ Countries stopped building big warships.
- Ⓑ People learned from the *Vasa*'s mistakes and built better ships.
- Ⓒ The country of Sweden was defeated in war.
- Ⓓ The builders of the ship were heroes throughout Sweden.

61. The shipwreck expert had no trouble gaining support for his plan. What does the phrase *gain support for* mean?
- Ⓐ to get people to agree with
- Ⓑ to take apart completely
- Ⓒ to be prepared for
- Ⓓ to carry out

62. Which statement best describes how the people of Sweden felt about the raising of the *Vasa*?
- Ⓐ They were excited.
- Ⓑ They were upset.
- Ⓒ They did not know about it.
- Ⓓ They did not care.

GO ON

Posttest

63. On the day the *Vasa* was raised, the country of Sweden "came to a halt." What does this mean?
    - Ⓐ People stopped doing what they usually did.
    - Ⓑ People went to bed in the middle of the day.
    - Ⓒ The electricity stopped working.
    - Ⓓ There was a sudden snowstorm.

64. Which of the following statements is true?
    - Ⓐ The *Vasa* was completely ruined after being under water for so long.
    - Ⓑ Once the *Vasa* was found, it took five more years to raise it.
    - Ⓒ The Vasa Museum is the most popular museum in the world.
    - Ⓓ The wider a boat is, the more likely it is to tip over.

65. Which event happened last in this article?
    - Ⓐ The *Vasa* Museum was built.
    - Ⓑ The *Vasa* was built.
    - Ⓒ The *Vasa* was recovered.
    - Ⓓ The *Vasa* sank.

66. Where do people go to see the *Vasa* warship today?
    - Ⓐ the United States
    - Ⓑ the bottom of Stockholm's harbor
    - Ⓒ the *Vasa* Museum
    - Ⓓ the Baltic Sea

67. How many people visit the *Vasa* each year?
    - Ⓐ almost eighty thousand
    - Ⓑ exactly eight hundred
    - Ⓒ more than a million
    - Ⓓ about eight hundred thousand

PART 1: ISAT for Reading
SESSION 3

68. The author would most likely agree with which of the following statements?

Ⓐ The *Vasa* should never have been built.

Ⓑ Swedish people do not know how to build boats.

Ⓒ The exact cause of the sinking of the *Vasa* is still a mystery.

Ⓓ Many people wasted their time by raising the *Vasa*.

69. What is the main purpose of this article?

Ⓐ to explain why the *Vasa* sank

Ⓑ to tell about the sinking and raising of the *Vasa*

Ⓒ to describe the history of Sweden's navy

Ⓓ to explain how sunken ships are raised

Posttest

Extended-Response Question

70. The sinking of the *Vasa* was a disaster. However, shipbuilders learned a lot from this disaster. As a result, they were able to build much better boats. What lessons do you think shipbuilders learned from the sinking of the *Vasa*?

_____

_____

_____

_____

_____

_____

_____

_____

_____

_____

_____

_____

End of PART 1: SESSION 3

STOP

Note to Students: Your written response will be scored using a rubric like the one on page 54.

PART 2: ISAT for Writing

ISAT for Writing

On the actual ISAT for Writing, you will be given only one thing to write about. You will not have a choice. On this practice test, however, you are given a choice. Be sure to read all three writing topics (the one below and the two on the next page) before you decide what to write about. Once you have chosen a topic, write a paper. You will have forty-five minutes.

Narrative Prompt

Think of a time when you were really excited about something. It might have been a school or club event that you were looking forward to, a party that you were invited to, or a trip that your family was planning. Describe how you felt before this event? What were you expecting? Did the event live up to your expectations? How did you feel after it was over?

OR

Note to Students: *If you respond to the narrative prompt, your written response will be scored using a rubric like the one on pages 55–57.*

Posttest

Persuasive Prompt

Imagine that your class sold the most raffle tickets for the school fundraiser. As a reward, your class gets to take a field trip. If you could go anywhere you wanted for the field trip, where would you want to go? Write a paper (essay) to persuade your teacher to take the class to the place that you would like to go for the field trip. Explain why this would be a good place to go for a field trip.

OR

Expository Prompt

Write a paper (essay) to explain to a younger person how to do something. For example, you might try to teach him or her how to tie a shoe, how to make a peanut butter and jelly sandwich, or how to fly a kite. Be sure to explain all the necessary steps.

End of PART 2: WRITING

Note to Students: *If you respond to the persuasive or expository prompt, your written response will be scored using a rubric like the one on pages 58–60.*

Glossary

Abbreviation. A shortened form of a word. Example: "Dr." instead of "doctor."

Achievement test. A test that measures what a student has learned. Compare with *aptitude test*.

Active reading. Thinking about what you are reading and becoming involved with it. **Active reading strategies** include asking questions, visualizing, predicting, summarizing, and making connections.

Alliteration. Consonant sounds that are repeated at the beginnings of words. Example: The m sound is repeated in "Molly and Mary and Maggie and me." Alliteration is one of the ways poets and writers use sound to create an effect in their writing.

Analyze. To look at all the parts of something and how they work together.

Aptitude test. A test that tries to measure a person's underlying ability or potential to do something. Compare with *achievement test*.

Arrangement. See *organization*.

Audience. Your readers—the people for whom you are writing.

Author. Writer.

Autobiography. The true story of a person's life, as told by that person. Compare with *biography*.

Base word. A complete word that can be joined with other word parts to form a new word. Example: suit + case = suitcase (*suit* and *case* are base words).

Biography. The true story of a person's life, as told by someone else. Compare with *autobiography*.

Blend. See *consonant cluster*.

Body. In an essay, the main part of the piece of writing. The body comes in the middle of an essay, after the introduction and before the conclusion. In the body, the writer presents ideas that support or develop the main idea that was stated in the introduction.

Boldface. Heavy, dark printing, like this: **This sentence is in boldface.**

Caption. Words next to or below a picture in the text. A caption tells readers about the picture.

Cause. The reason why something happens, such as an event that makes something else happen. Compare with *effect*.

Cause-and-effect order. One way to organize ideas in a piece of writing. Causes may be followed by effects, or effects may be followed by causes.

Cause-and-effect question. A question about causes and effects.

Character. A person or animal that takes part in the action of a story.

Chart. A type of graphic organizer. Information is shown in rows (going across) and columns (going up and down). See *graphic organizer*.

Checklist. A list of things to do. Items on the list should be checked off as they are completed. Example: the Revision Checklist on page 211.

Chronological order. See *time order*.

Classroom test. A test that measures what students in a class have recently learned about a particular subject. Compare with *general test*.

Clincher sentence. A sentence at or near the end of a paragraph. This sentence summarizes or otherwise ends the paragraph. Also called a *concluding sentence*.

Cluster chart. See *word web*.

Comparison. Showing the ways in which two or more things are alike (or not). See *contrast*.

Comparison-and-contrast order. Another way to organize ideas in a piece of writing. Similarities may be followed by differences, or differences may be followed by similarities.

Comparison-and-contrast question. A question about similarities and differences.

Comprehension. Understanding something. Example: Reading comprehension questions test whether you understand the meaning of what you have just read.

Concluding sentence. See *clincher sentence*.

Conclusion. The end. The last part of an essay or long piece of writing. In an essay, the conclusion often summarizes the important ideas or states the writer's main point (thesis) in a different way.

Conflict. A big problem faced by a character, especially the main character. Sometimes called the *central conflict*. The conflict may involve a struggle with another character.

Connecting. An active reading strategy. See *making connections*.

Connecting words. See *transitions*.

Consonant. Sounds such as /p/, /f/, /m/, /s/, and /w/ that are formed by certain movements of the mouth, lips, or tongue. Consonants include all the letters of the alphabet except the vowels *a, e, i, o, u,* and sometimes *y*.

Consonant cluster. Two or more consonants used together, such as *br, sn,* or *nch*. See *blend, digraph,* and *trigraph*.

Context. The words surrounding another word or group of words. If you are not sure of the meaning of a word, you can often figure it out from the clues in its context. See *context clue*.

Context clue. In a reading selection, words, usually nearby, that can help you to figure out what a new or unfamiliar word means.

Contrast. Showing the ways in which two or more things are different or opposite.

Conventions. In writing, the rules for using capital letters and punctuation marks. Some people also include the rules for indenting paragraphs and margins, underlining book titles, and so on as conventions. See also *manuscript form, mechanics*.

Degree order. See *order of importance*.

Describe. To show, in a piece of writing (or speech), how something looks, feels, smells, tastes, or sounds. See also *sensory details*.

Descriptive writing. Writing that uses words to create a picture of something in your mind.

Detail. A specific piece of information. Example: A fact about a particular person, place, or idea would be a detail. A *significant detail* is an important piece of information. See also *sensory details, supporting details*.

Diary. See *journal*.

Digraph. A single sound spelled with two letters, such as *ph, sh,* and *th.*

Directions. Step-by-step instructions that tell you what to do and how to do it. See also *writing prompt.*

Drafting. An early part of the writing process, before the writing is in final form. When you write a rough draft, you just try to get your ideas down on paper. See also *final draft, rough draft.*

Drama. A play that is meant to be performed by actors, usually on stage. Examples: screenplays for movies and television shows, stage plays.

Effect. An event or result that is caused by one or more other events. Compare with *cause.*

Elaboration. 1. Providing additional ideas or information to support an idea, point of view, or description. Writers elaborate by including specific details, examples, facts, opinions, paraphrases, quotations, reasons, and summaries. 2. In a paragraph, any statement that supports a topic sentence or thesis statement. See *supporting details, thesis.*

Essay. A piece of nonfiction writing that is more than one paragraph long. An essay explores a single part of a subject—a certain topic.

Evaluating. Judging whether something is good or bad, right or wrong, strong or weak. When you evaluate a piece of writing, you judge how well it was written.

Event. Something that happens.

Example. Something that is chosen to show what a more general idea or group is like. A particular instance (person, place, or idea) that is typical of a larger group with similar characteristics. Examples are a good way to support, or back up, ideas in a piece of writing. Examples can also provide context clues to the meaning of words. See also *context clue, supporting details.*

Exclamation point. A punctuation mark (like this: !) used at the end of a sentence that expresses strong feeling.

Explain. To tell how or why, by giving reasons, causes, examples, or other details. See also *elaboration, support.*

Extended-response question. A question that requires a fairly long answer. Sometimes, the answer must use evidence from one or more readings. See also *open-response question.*

Fable. A short tale with animal characters that is told to teach a moral, or lesson. See also *folktale, moral.*

Fact. A detail or statement that can be proved to be true. Compare with *opinion.*

Fiction. A story about imaginary characters, places, and events. Compare with *nonfiction.*

Final draft. A finished version of a piece of writing, especially one that has been revised and proofread. Compare with *rough draft.*

Five-paragraph theme. An essay that is five paragraphs long, with an introduction, three body paragraphs, and a conclusion. Sometimes called a *standard classroom theme.*

Focused. 1. On track—related to the topic. Example: A piece of writing is focused if the writer does not wander onto other topics. 2. Narrowed or targeted on something specific. Example: A topic is focused if it is narrower and more specific than a more general subject.

Folktale. A story that has been passed down over many years from older people to younger people by word of mouth. See also *fable*.

Function. What something does—its purpose. See also *purpose*.

General test. A test, often given at or near the end of the year, that measures a broad range of skills students have learned up to that point (during the year and in previous grades).

Grammar. The rules that tell how words and word parts can be combined into phrases and sentences.

Graphic organizer. A chart, word web, timeline, or other type of picture used for taking notes or for organizing and showing ideas. You can also use a graphic organizer to gather ideas for a piece of writing.

Heading. A subhead (or section title) that appears within a reading selection.

History. 1. The study of the past. 2. A true story about the past.

Illustration. A picture. Example: a drawing, photograph, or map.

Image. In writing, a word or phrase (group of words) that names something that can be seen, heard, touched, tasted, or smelled. Writers often use *sensory details* to create images.

Informative writing. Nonfiction writing that gives facts or information on a subject. Also called *expository writing*.

Integration. Keeping it together; explaining or expressing ideas in such a way that they hang together, flow smoothly, and make sense.

Introduction. The beginning. The first part of a story, an essay, or long piece of writing. In an essay, the introduction usually tells the main idea, or thesis. See also *thesis*.

Italics. Slanted type, like this: *This sentence is in italics.*

Journal. A notebook where you write down or record, day by day, your thoughts, events in your life, or anything else that you want to write about. Also called a *diary*.

Key words. The most important words in a selection or in a question about a selection.

Lead. See *opening*.

Leader line. See *multiple-choice question*, *opening*.

Learning log. See *reading log*.

Main character. The most important character in a story.

Main idea. 1. The most important idea in a paragraph or piece of writing. In an essay or a longer piece of nonfiction writing, each paragraph usually will focus on a main idea. 2. The main point the writer wants to make, sometimes called the thesis. See also *thesis*.

Making connections. Thinking about how something you have read or heard is related to something in your own life or to something else that you already know about. Making connections is an active reading strategy. See also *prior knowledge*.

Manuscript form. The way a piece of writing is presented on paper. Examples: Manuscript form includes proper spacing between words and lines, width of margins, and paragraph indentations. It also includes underlining of book titles and correct placement of titles, headings, captions, page numbers, and so on. For student papers, manuscript form often includes the writer's name and class and the date.

Mechanics. The "nuts and bolts" of writing. Punctuation and capitalization.

Moral. The lesson contained in a story, especially one that tells how people should or should not think or behave. See also *fable*.

Multiple-choice question. A question that begins with an opening part, or leader line, and provides a list of three or four answer choices. See also *opening*.

Myth. A story about gods or goddesses.

Narrative. A story, which may be true (nonfiction) or imaginary (fiction).

Narrator. The person who tells a story.

Negative words. Words like *not* or *except*. When used in a multiple-choice question, words like this are an important clue to how you should go about choosing the answer.

Nonfiction. Writing about real people, places, and events. Compare with *fiction*.

Note. A quick reminder you have jotted down about something you have heard or read. Notes are words and phrases (groups of words), not full sentences. See also *notetaking*.

Notetaking. Jotting down or recording important ideas and information from something you have heard or read. Notes may be taken in outline form or in some type of chart or graphic organizer.

Onomatopoeia. Words that sound like what they mean. Examples: *buzz, meow*.

Opening. 1. In a multiple-choice question, the first part (*leader line*), before the list of answer choices. Examples: Sometimes the opening is a question. Sometimes it contains a blank to be filled in. Sometimes it is a sentence that is to be completed by the correct answer from the list of choices below it. 2. The first line at the beginning of a piece of writing, especially an introductory paragraph. Writers usually try to begin with an opening that will grab their readers' attention. Also called a *lead*.

Open-response question. A question that asks you to come up with your own answer. The answer may be a paragraph or a complete essay. See also *extended-response question*.

Opinion. A statement that cannot be proved to be true or false. Compare with *fact*.

Order of importance. A type of organization in which ideas or details are arranged from most important to least important or from least important to most important.

Organization. The way something is set up or arranged. In a piece of writing, organization is the way the writer arranges his or her ideas and details. Examples: *order of importance, spatial order, time order*.

Outline. See *rough outline*.

Paragraph. A group of sentences, usually about a single main idea. A **standard paragraph** includes a topic sentence that states the main idea, two or more supporting sentences, and a clincher (concluding) sentence.

Persuasive writing. Writing that expresses opinions or takes a position on something. It asks readers to adopt or share the writer's viewpoint or to take some type of action in response to the ideas expressed in the writing.

Phonics. The study of the sounds that make up words. See also *blend, consonant, digraph, trigraph,* and *vowels.*

Phrase. A short group of words that work together. Examples: *in the morning, over there,* and *the big, blue balloon.*

Poetry. Words used in an unusual way to get across an idea or an experience more powerfully than it would be expressed in everyday speech or writing. Poems are written in lines of verse instead of paragraphs. Poets use the sounds of words to create effects.

Predicting. Guessing what will happen in the future. Predicting what will happen next is an active reading strategy.

Prefix. A word part that is added to the beginning of a word to form a new word. Example: *anti* + *social* = *antisocial.*

Prereading. See *previewing.*

Previewing. What a reader can do before reading a selection carefully. Previewing includes scanning the parts, thinking what you already know about the topic, and asking questions. This process is also called *prereading.* See also *scanning.*

Prewriting. Getting ready to write about something. Prewriting is the part of the writing process in which you choose a topic, gather ideas, and organize your ideas.

Prior knowledge. What you already know about a subject.

Process. Anything that involves more than one step. A process takes place over a certain amount of time. It also involves changes from one step to the next. See also *writing process.*

Prompt. See *writing prompt.*

Proofreading. Looking over a piece of writing to find and correct any errors in spelling, grammar, usage, punctuation, and capitalization.

Publishing. Sharing your writing with others. Examples: giving copies to your friends, family, classmates, or teacher; reading your writing aloud; or posting it on a classroom billboard or Web site.

Purpose. In writing, what a writer wants his or her writing to do. Examples: A writer's purpose may be to describe, to explain, to entertain, to inform, or to persuade.

Questioning. Asking about something. A question often begins with *who, what, where, when, why,* or *how.* Asking questions before or as you read a selection (and noticing how they are answered later on) is an active reading strategy.

Reading comprehension. Understanding what you read.

Reading log. A notebook or journal where you record, usually day by day, what you have read, both in your homework for school and on your own, just for fun.

Reflecting. Thinking about what you have just heard or read.

Responding. Not only thinking about what you are hearing or reading but also reacting to it.

Revising. Making changes to improve a piece of writing. Examples: making the content (ideas and details) more interesting or accurate, rearranging the order of ideas and details, or getting rid of unnecessary details.

note(s), 118, 180
notetaking, 118, 180–84; symbols and abbreviations, 184

O
onomatopoeia, 172
opinion, 156
order, of importance, 206; spatial, 206; time, 206
organizing, 206
outline. *See* rough outline

P
paragraph(s), 219–26; standard, 222; writing for tests, 226
persuasive essay, ISAT rubric for, 58–60; nonfiction, 154; writing, 256–58
phrase, 182
poetry, 155
predicting, 107, 108
prefix(es), 93–94
prereading, 106
previewing, 101, 106
prewriting, 201, 218
prior knowledge, 106
process, 200
proofreading, 201, 213, 218
proofreading checklist, 213
publishing, 201, 218
purpose, 156

Q
questioning, 107, 108, 109

R
reading actively, 100–21
reading comprehension, 122–52

reading skills, review, 61–172
reflecting, 119
responding, 119
revising, 201, 210, 218
revision and proofreading symbols, 214
revision checklist, 211
rhyme, 172
rhythm, 172
root(s), 97
rough draft, 209
rough outline, 183, 196, 207, 231, 241
rubrics, 54–60

S
scanning, 101
schwa sound, 90
sensory detail, 205
sentence(s), clincher, 219, 220; concluding, 220; supporting, 220; topic, 220, 222
sequence, 124, 133; questions about, 134
setting, 163
short vowels, 76
significant detail, 129; questions about, 130
sounds, 69–98
spatial order, 206
spellings of sounds, 69–98
standard paragraph, 222
strategies, test-taking, 38–60
subhead, 101
suffix(es), 95–96
summarizing, 107, 109, 111, 119, 243
supporting detail, 219–26
supporting sentences, 220

syllable(s), 92
symbol, 182, 184

T
test(s), classroom, 38; general, 39; getting ready for, 39
text, 101
theme, 124, 146–47, 164; questions about, 148
thesis, 156, 228
thesis statement, 155, 231
timeline, 188–89
time order, 206, 221
title, 101
topic, 155, 203; narrowing, 203
topic sentence, 219, 220, 222
transitions, 220–21, 226
trigraph, 75

V
visualizing, 107, 108
vocabulary, 124, 142
vowel(s), 76–90; long and short, 76

W
word(s), base, 92
word-analysis question(s), 52
word parts, 69–98, 142
word web, 120, 186–87
writing, 195–258; expository, 154, 253–55; informative, 154, 253–55; about literature, 245–47; narrative, 154, 250–52; persuasive, 154, 256–58; process, 201–18; prompt, 53, 196, 202; rubrics, 54–60

Index

A
abbreviation, 181, 182, 184
active reading, 99–121; strategies, 107
alliteration, 172
author, 101
autobiography, 154

B
base word, 92
biography, 154
blend, 74
body, 228, 240–41

C
caption, 101
cause(s), 124, 137, 221
causes and effect(s), 137–38; questions about, 139
central conflict, 163
character(s), main, 163
chart, 190–91
classroom test, 38
clincher sentence, 219, 220
comparing, 96, 221
comprehend, 52
concluding sentence, 220
conclusion, 228, 243
conflict, central, 163
connections, making, 107, 109–11
consonant(s), 70–75; blend, 74; cluster, 74; digraphs, 75; hard and soft, 72; initial, medial, and final, 70; silent, 75; trigraphs, 75
context clue(s), 142–44; questions about, 144
contrasting, 221
CVC words, 76

D
detail(s), 183; sensory, 205; significant, 129; supporting, 219–26
diary, 40
digraph, 75
diphthong, 87
drafting, 201, 209, 218
drama, 155

E
edit, 210
effect(s), 124, 137, 221
essay(s), 47, 228–44
evaluating, 119, 201, 210, 218
events, 163
expository essay, 53; ISAT rubric for, 58–60; nonfiction, 154; writing, 253–55
extended-response question(s), 47, 52; ISAT rubric for, 54

F
fact, 156
fiction, 154, 163; reading, 163–72
final consonants, 70
final draft, 197

G
general test, 39
graphic organizer(s), 186–94; chart, 190–91; timeline, 188–89; word web, 120, 186–87

H
heading, 101
history, 154

I
illustration, 101
informative essay, ISAT rubric for, 58–60; nonfiction, 154; writing, 253–55
initial consonants, 70
introduction, 101, 228, 236
ISAT for Reading, 52; extended-response rubric, 54
ISAT for Writing, 53; rubrics, 55–60

J
journal, 40

K
key words, 101, 130

L
literature, writing about, 245–47
long vowels, 76

M
main character, 163
main idea(s), 124–26, 155, 203, 219–26; questions about, 126
medial consonants, 70
multiple-choice question(s), 43, 52; answering, 45

N
narrative essay, ISAT rubric for, 55–57
narrative nonfiction, 154; writing, 250–52
negative words, 45
nonfiction, 154; reading, 153–62

Text. Any type of reading material. Examples: books, magazine articles, stories, Web pages.

Theme. The lesson a story teaches; the writer's message. You can often figure out the theme by paying attention to what the main character learns by the end of a story.

Thesis. The main idea in a piece of nonfiction writing such as an essay. The writer often states this idea in a *thesis statement*, which typically appears in the introduction of an essay or longer piece of writing. The rest of the essay or piece of writing develops this idea.

Thesis statement. A brief statement (in one or two sentences) of the main idea. See also *main idea, thesis*.

Time order. The order in which events happen. Also called *chronological order*.

Timeline. A graphic organizer that shows when important events happened by showing dates above or below the years on a number line. You can also use a timeline to take notes about when things happened.

Title. The name of a piece of writing. The title usually appears at the beginning of the piece.

Topic. What a writer has chosen to write about; usually a narrower, more focused part of a broader subject.

Topic sentence. In a paragraph, a sentence that tells the main idea.

Transitions. Words or phrases (groups of words) that show how ideas are connected. Transitions can be used to connect ideas within a paragraph or one paragraph to the next. Examples: *first, then, next, finally,* and *as a result*.

Trigraph. A single sound spelled with three letters, such as *ght* and *tle*.

Visualizing. Picturing something in your mind as you listen or read about it. Visualizing is an active reading strategy.

Vocabulary. 1. All the words a person (or a group of people) knows. 2. A list of words, especially new or unfamiliar words from a reading selection.

Voice. The unique sound of a piece of writing. Voice is created by a writer's style, which includes not only the choice of words but the way they are presented.

Vowels. The sounds /a/, /e/, /i/, /o/, and /u/. The letters that stand for these sounds.

Word-analysis question. A question that tests your ability to use phonics and your knowledge of word parts to recognize words and word patterns.

Word parts. *Base words, roots,* and the *prefixes* or *suffixes* that can be added to them to make other words.

Word web. A type of graphic organizer that shows details or related ideas clustered around one main idea at the center. First you write down the main idea and circle it. Then you gather more ideas or details and draw lines to connect them to the main idea. Also called a *cluster chart*.

Writing process. The steps involved in producing a finished piece of writing: *prewriting, drafting, revising, proofreading,* and *publishing*.

Writing prompt. A set of directions or instructions for doing a piece of writing, especially on a test.

Rhyme. Repeated sounds at the ends of words. Example: Under the *June moon* the *loon crooned* a *tune*.

Rhythm. The pattern of strong and weak beats in a poem or song.

Root. A main word part that is not a complete word by itself but that can be joined with other word parts to make new words. Example: *tele* + graph = telegraph.

Rough draft. An early version of a piece of writing that is not finished yet. Compare with *final draft*.

Rough outline. A quick list of main ideas and supporting ideas or details. In an outline, main ideas are written at the left margin, and details are written in a list underneath each main idea. Supporting ideas are usually introduced by dashes.

Rubric. A list of scoring guidelines or an explanation of the standards for judging a piece of writing or some other work project.

Scanning. Looking over a reading selection quickly to preview the parts and get a general idea of what the piece is about.

Schwa. The schwa sound /ə/ sounds like "uh." It can be spelled with all the vowels in English. Example: The *a* in *sofa* is a schwa sound.

Sensory details. Details that help to create a vivid picture of something by appealing to the reader's senses. Examples: Things you can see, feel, smell, hear, or taste.

Sentence. A group of words that is grammatically correct and states a complete idea. In a **run-on sentence,** too many ideas are jammed into the same sentence. In a **sentence fragment,** the thought is incomplete. Something (a subject or verb) is missing, so the group of words is not a complete sentence.

Sequence. The order of events in a piece of writing.

Setting. The time and place in which the action of a story takes place.

Spatial order. A type of organization in which ideas or details are arranged by location, from near to far, left to right, top to bottom, front to back, or the opposite.

Subhead. See *heading*.

Suffix. A word part that is added to the end of a word to form a new word. Example: hope + *ful* = hopeful.

Summarizing. To say again, in fewer (and different) words, what something you heard or read was about. Summarizing is an active reading strategy.

Support. To explain or illustrate an idea, or back up a point.

Supporting details. Details that explain or illustrate a main idea. Supporting details may include examples, facts, opinions, or other details that support, or back up, the main idea. See also *elaboration*.

Supporting sentences. In a paragraph, the sentences that back up or give more information about the topic sentence.

Syllable. A part of a word that forms a single sound. A syllable is usually made up of a vowel and one or more consonants around it. There are as many syllables in a word as there are vowel sounds.

Symbol. 1. Something that stands for another thing besides itself. Example: A rose is a traditional symbol of love and beauty. 2. A special mark that stands for something beyond itself, such as + or & for the word *and*.